S0-AFK-331

THE DIVERSITY HOAX

Law Students Report From Berkeley

Edited by
David Wienir and Marc Berley

Foundation for
Academic Standards
& Tradition

New York, New York

Foundation for
Academic Standards
& Tradition

FAST – Foundation for Academic Standards & Tradition
545 Madison Avenue
New York, NY 10022

THE DIVERSITY HOAX Copyright © 1999 by David Wienir and Marc Berley
All rights reserved. No part of this book may be used or reproduced in any
manner whatsoever without written permission except in the case of brief
quotations embodied in critical articles and reviews.

This publication has not been authorized or endorsed by the University of
California, Berkeley. The views expressed here are solely those of the authors
and editors.

To purchase additional copies of this book, please call (800) 247-6553.
For further information, please visit FAST's Web site at http://www.gofast.org.

Design: James Robie Design Associates

Cover photo: Sather Gate / The Bancroft Library,
University of California, Berkeley
UARC PIC 24B:6

Manufactured in the United States of America

ISBN 0-9669940-0-0

To students everywhere

Introduction
By Marc Berley

This book is the result of the efforts of one first-year law student. In his first months as a student at the University of California, Berkeley School of Law (Boalt Hall), David Wienir was startled by the lack of intellectual diversity he found among students, professors, and administrators. What is more, he was first dismayed and later terrified by the lack of intellectual freedom to be found in classrooms, hallways, and courtyards. David encountered something he had not expected to find at a "top-ten" law school – inconceivable intolerance for any views that did not accord with what appeared to be the prevailing campus view on Proposition 209.[1] Although it was voted on by the people of California, David found many on campus acting as if Proposition 209 carried none of the moral power of the law and had to be reversed by any means necessary.

David was not naive when he applied to Berkeley; he knew that radical liberal politics rule the roost at most American ivory towers – and especially Berkeley. He could not believe that an elite American law school could actually turn its back on the tradition that, from the time of Cicero, had lawyers train by learning to argue *in utrimque parte*, speaking on both sides of every issue. David did not expect his

---

[1] The California Civil Rights Initiative, also known as Proposition 209, was passed on November 5, 1996 by 54 percent of California voters. Proposition 209 ended the practice of racial preference in admissions policies at the University of California, Berkeley. See Appendix A.

classmates to hold his view on controversial topics such as racial preference, but he did not expect to find classes disrupted and to be
called names merely for holding his opinion, and pretty much keeping it to himself. As David describes it, the problem was that 'diversity' protesters were intimidating diverse students in the name of
diversity. The protesters wanted David, among others, to sign an
anti-Proposition 209 petition, and the more often David politely
refused to sign, the more fiercely he was maligned, accused, and
called offensive names.

David's first few months at Boalt Hall were rough ones.
Nevertheless, he kept his poise and remained optimistic. Hoping to
find that there was more intellectual freedom and diversity at Boalt
Hall than he himself had experienced, he set himself a project. He
sent out a letter to every student at Boalt suggesting they submit
essays that he would try to publish as *The Berkeley Federalist Law
Papers*, a nonpartisan publication dedicated to open and honest
expression. The call for papers asked some simple questions: "How
healthy is the marketplace of ideas here at Boalt? Do you have fair
opportunity to share your ideas in the classroom? Does expression
flow freely in an environment tolerant of diversity, or does the climate of tolerance at Berkeley paradoxically inhibit true diversity of
opinion? Has political activism within the classroom silenced important student perspectives?" Seeking "diary-like" submissions, David
made it clear that "all viewpoints are welcome and encouraged."
"Let your voice be heard," he wrote.[2] And he kept his word. In the
spirit of free speech, this book reprints all of the submissions David
received.

The Diversity Hoax is a book of essays by Berkeley law students:
women, men, minorities, Democrats, Republicans, and moderates
alike – and different. While their backgrounds, life experiences,
political views, and physical characteristics are different, their views
on intellectual freedom at Berkeley are starkly similar: diversity – different points of view – is not, by and large, to be found on campus,
chiefly because it is neither encouraged nor supported. Regardless of

---

[2] See "The Question," reprinted below.

background, many of the students published in this book see themselves, with considerable authority, as part of a true minority at Berkeley – those who are not only willing to tolerate opposing views but who know that only "a free and open marketplace of ideas benefits all."

This is an honest book, recounting in vivid, authoritative detail the experiences of UC Berkeley law students during a year in which intimidating 'diversity' protesters did much to ruin the experience of many students. As a number of contributors recount in the pages that follow, the protesters harassed not only those who did not agree with them, but also those who merely decided not to support them openly (that is, with an activist's fervor).

There is no pretense in these pages. The students who submitted essays to David did so because they perceived a problem they wanted to describe to the world. Berkeley was famous for fighting for free speech in the 1960's. But, as the contributors describe here, the academic year of 1997-98 saw the successful silencing of many students who sought diversity of ideas and free speech. The 'diversity' protesters and petitioners (a fluctuating group of students generally ranging from 20 to 100) used bullying tactics – tactics so ugly, as these pages tell, that liberal and moderate Democrats alike felt silenced by the radical liberals with whom they thought they shared a belief in fairness and freedom of speech.

The essays in this book are not the burnished policy pieces of professional writers. While some are polished, others are raw and heartfelt. All of them are subjective and urgent. Read together, these essays paint a compelling portrait of the state of free speech at one of America's top law schools.

All but two of the submissions David received report that a diversity of ideas is not encouraged at Berkeley. The most noticeable hypocrisy at Berkeley, the contributors make clear, is that, for the majority, diversity has to do only with skin color, not with ideas. Free speech is in jeopardy. Politically correct ("PC") thought-police censor. In too many awful scenarios, PC racism prevails.

One of the most grievous tactics of the 'diversity' protesters' prolonged campaign was to disrupt classes by bringing in minority stu-

dents from outside the Boalt community. After acting rudely to professors, the protesters would then confront white students and ask
them in a forceful way to give up their seats to a minority student –
a symbolic gesture. But in at least one case, the 'diversity' protesters
unwittingly asked a minority student and refused to tolerate her dissenting view. As one woman who cares greatly about both intellectual and racial diversity tells in some of the most riveting pages of this
book, she herself, although a minority of mixed race, was called
repugnant, indeed racist, names simply on account of the views she
held. "When I expressed my outrage at being asked to give up my
seat to a minority at a recent classroom protest staged in support of
affirmative action," writes Isabelle Quinn, "this caused a classmate to
call me a 'racist white conservative idiot.'"

PC racism has been blind to its various victims in recent years.
Many of the essays here document how hypocritical, self-centered,
and intolerant the 'diversity' protesters could be. But that's what
happens when people put their feelings before other people's facts.
One would not think that people who worship at the altar of identity politics would assert their right to declare their "group" without
affording other people the same right, but that is what often happens. The 'diversity' protestors, after all, do not ask everyone they
harass for a family tree. Of course, we would not want them to, and
that's the point. Wishing to be outwardly proud of their "group" or
ethnicity, however, they don't allow true individuals to be quiet about
theirs. There is also that other problem of not respecting people who
actually happen to be and consider themselves white.

As every student of civil rights in America should know, bullying tactics can keep justice at bay for only so long. A dedicated student of Western civilization, Martin Luther King, Jr. had absolute
beliefs about justice that he would not violate – that was his power.
Unfortunately, many of today's students are indoctrinated warriors,
taught by radical professors to reject the best of what the Western tradition has to offer and mistake power for justice. Not coincidental-
ly, they mistake polite dissent for usurpation of their power. It is sad
to see so many of America's students pushed in the direction of intolerance, pessimism, and confrontation rather than in the direction of

tolerance, hope, and peace.

Racism still exists in America. Thirty-five years after the Civil Rights Act of 1964, however, America has much reason for optimism. America has been and remains committed to eradicating institutional racism. Unfortunately, new forms of resistance to a color-blind society are increasingly evident. In an atmosphere in which the color of skin has come to matter more than the content of character or demonstrated skills, Proposition 209 reasserts the language of that momentous Civil Rights Act of 1964. Opposition to Proposition 209, however, especially on the UC Berkeley campus, has demonstrated a determination by some to defer the dream of a color-blind society. Anti-American sentiment, refusal to assimilate, and separatist ethnic identity politics do untold damage to our schools and to our country, generally harming minorities most of all.

Now is not the time to sanction reverse discrimination and institutionalized racism. That, at least, was the view of California when it voted on Proposition 209. Even if students disagree with the people of California, now is not the time to sanction the silencing of democratic debate about controversial topics, especially at universities, where intellectual freedom is invaluable.

This book is not a joy to publish. It documents some of the worst educational trends currently threatening our country. According to the immediate needs of the "liberal" revolution on campus, ideas come to substitute for skin color, and skin color comes to substitute for ideas. In this charged atmosphere, many of America's most successful minorities – Ward Connerly, Thomas Sowell, and Clarence Thomas, to take just a few examples – are vilified on university campuses as traitors or puppets, rather than accepted (or merely tolerated) as successful individuals who are free to espouse their views. Although these black intellectuals have arrived at their diverse views through life experience and considerable study, their experience and hard work do not matter to the 'diversity' protestors who disagree with them. To many opponents of Proposition 209, minorities who oppose racial preference "think white" and hence are white – at least for the purposes of the 'diversity' revolution. By the same token, repugnant pejorative names are slung at minorities who hold anything resembling conservative views.

These are some of the sad facts at the center of the diversity hoax. To the 'diversity' protesters, only some facts matter. Only some efforts count. Only some opinions are acceptable. And all ideas are reducible to race.

I continue to put the word *diversity* in single quotation marks when referring to the protesters because, as the essays here demonstrate, diversity is coming to mean whatever the 'diversity' protesters say it means. And whoever says otherwise is hastily silenced and excluded from diversity. As Humpty Dumpty says to Alice in *Through the Looking Glass*, "When I use a word, it means just what I choose it to mean – neither more nor less." So the 'diversity' protesters would have it, but the word *diversity* means many different things to different people.

The biggest problem expressed in the essays here is that because diversity of opinion is stifled at Berkeley, students – all students – are not learning as much as they could in their classrooms. Students from across the political spectrum form what has become a silenced minority – students who understand that the end of free speech and intellectual freedom, in the service of whatever revolution, means the destruction of education, individualism, and any semblance of the American dream.

In the 1960's, Berkeley was the famous center of the Free Speech Movement in America. People dedicated to free speech came from all around the country to be a part of the movement led by Mario Savio. Savio died in 1996. One year later free speech began to die at UC Berkeley. In the 1997-98 academic year, Berkeley became a place where free speech was attacked by harassing protesters. As the students who contributed to this volume recount, the 'diversity' protesters not only worked to curtail the free speech of students who disagreed with their position on racial preference; they also intimidated students who early supported them but who, after joining in, came to question the protesters' intolerant tactics.

The 1997-98 academic year was a sad chapter in free speech at Berkeley. True liberalism gave way to an impulse to accomplish a mission by illiberal means. As David Wienir observes in "The

History," the great liberal John Stuart Mill would not have been happy to witness the recent silencing of minority views at Berkeley. "All silencing of discussion," wrote Mill, is a dangerous "assumption of infallibility."

Students who have always fought to protect the free speech of others found themselves confronting hostile methods to silence their views at Berkeley. "Funny, I've always thought of myself as a classic liberal – the type that defends vociferously the rights of people to disagree with me," writes Nick-Anthony Buford in "What Ever Happened to John Stuart Mill?" But, "ironically, the inspiring 'traditional' 1960's paradigm of Berkeley – of respect for diverse opinions – is subverted, and trampled by the new intolerance of the activist student thought-police who police the discussions which take place in the classrooms and hallways." In "News from the Ladies' Room," Megan Elizabeth Murray holds "the belief that we all have a right to speak." But at Boalt, she points out, "the very people whose rights I was trying to respect were not respecting the rights of others."

When the mind is fettered, it is not free to grow. When intellectual freedom is denied to some, everyone loses, as the contributors to this book make clear. "In my module, in particular, there exists a great deal of unease between the Right and the Left," writes Randall Lewis in "We're All Losers." "I sympathize with the Left much more often. Yet, that does not imply that I won't make comments that I regard as theoretically true when an argument on the Left is weak. Hindering speech and refraining from making logical points only works to all our detriment," writes Lewis. "It is important that students on both sides do not sneer at or mock other students."

As Heather McCormick writes in "The Unprofitable Monopoly," "many who disagree with the ultra-liberal viewpoint that dominates discussion at Boalt have learned to keep silent." Wondering how this could be the case at a top law school, she asks: "Why is it that we, as advocates in training, are nevertheless so reluctant to stand up for our positions?" Like many others raised in this book, it is a material question. "Our expectations are anchored so far to the Left at Boalt," writes McCormick, that "in most classes, we don't hear from true conservatives at all, only less extreme liberals."

McCormick's proposed solution to the problem would demand more of conservatives and liberals alike: "More conservatives must be willing to express their viewpoints in class, in spite of their fears of being demonized. Should the debate become one-sided nevertheless, more liberals and moderates need to offer alternative perspectives, even if that means playing devil's advocate."

It is a reasonable proposal, but Boalt Hall, as these essays demonstrate, has a long way to go. On her first day of school, writes Darcy Edmonds, "I feared confrontation with fellow students asking me to carry signs and demonstrate for a cause about which I was still unsure." Soon, however, Edmonds writes, "I agreed with [the protesters'] intention of showing that the students were united in their belief in diversity in the classroom, so I agreed to participate." Edmonds soon noticed the duplicity of the protesters, who did not tell all their supporters the full extent and intolerant nature of their plans. Instead, she saw their ability "for using...other students like pawns in their game of political strategy." Where did this leave her? "I felt I could not tell anyone my personal philosophies – that I wanted to increase opportunities for students of diverse backgrounds but did not support affirmative action." The harassing tactics of the 'diversity' protesters created an atmosphere in which students were "not willing to risk resentment by voicing their honest opinions." The diversity hoax – the hoodwinking assumption that diversity includes only certain views – was terrifying.

The students printed here ask some numbing questions, questions American higher education would do well to confront with honesty. "What was I thinking expecting a mature public discussion in a top U.S. law school?" writes Murray. "To me," she writes, "diversity is a range of viewpoints and experiences." Murray asks further, "How can we 'become' color-blind all the while highlighting our differences with fireworks? We end up pitted against each other based on race instead of forgetting that we look different. To advance we must advance ourselves. Each of us must stop complaining about the past and look to the future."

The purpose of this book is to allow students not merely to express their views, but also to express in a meaningful way the difficulty they have faced trying to express them at UC Berkeley.

The circumstances of the publication of this book by FAST are particularly important. The Foundation for Academic Standards & Tradition is a nonpartisan, not-for-profit organization created to empower diverse college and university students nationwide to restore both high academic standards and humanistic study of the liberal arts in the Western tradition to their schools. FAST works to reverse the tragic "dumbing down" and irresponsible politicization in evidence at so many schools across the country. FAST was founded because many students understand the value of the Western intellectual tradition and the necessity of raising academic standards in American institutions of higher learning.* Without common ground, students from increasingly diverse backgrounds will not learn to speak and listen to one another. Now, more than ever, it is imperative that American educators make sure that students read a collection of books that will help make them informed critical thinkers with common ground. At the same time, schools must encourage intellectual freedom. FAST is dedicated to the pursuit of free speech for student voices. This is why FAST is publishing the essays that follow. As McCormick writes in her thoughtful essay, the "silencing of dissenting voices at Boalt also means that our classroom discussions are much less rich than they might otherwise be."

What is occurring at Berkeley appears to be a decline in academic standards that is connected to a concerted effort on the part of professors and students to reject the Western tradition. The essays here suggest that the pursuit of truth rooted in reason is being replaced by a rejection of reason as a mere tool of oppression, rather than the valuable source of self-correction that, in America, led visionary white men to abolish slavery.

It is under such conditions that Shakespeare becomes known as the cultural artifact of an oppressive culture, rather than a fine poet who has much to teach diverse people about human nature. Under such conditions, Western civilization is wrongly attacked, made responsible for all of the world's ills, but ignored where it has led the

---

* Editors' Note: See Appendix B.

way in confronting and lessening those ills. When pursued with honesty, history shows, the Western intellectual tradition leads to recognition of errors and a determination to accomplish self-correction. Conversely, many countries and cultures that have done neither are the pets of the 'diversity' protesters and their demands for a multicultural curriculum based on vague and hyperbolic notions of egalitarianism and social engineering.

Racial preference, it is the reasoned belief of many, and the belief of a majority of Californians who voted on Proposition 209, is not only unjust but also harmful to both individuals and institutions of higher learning. Lowering admissions criteria for some helps no one. I myself would like to see more black students attend elite universities, including UC Berkeley. The best way to improve the opportunities for all students, I believe, is truly to raise standards in K-12 education and apply college admissions criteria fairly. A challenging course of action, but more promising than racial preferences.

This is not, however, a book about Proposition 209. It is a book about free speech and intellectual freedom – a book in which students recount the obstacles they confronted when they expressed their views on a number of controversial topics at UC Berkeley. David Wienir was my student in his first year as an undergraduate at Columbia University. Together with a diverse group of bright, curious, and tolerant students in my humanities course, David helped all of us to explore the wonderful controversies embedded in books by writers such as Homer, Plato, Dante, Shakespeare, and Jane Austen. Now, six years later, David has helped all of us consider more deeply one of the most controversial issues facing us today.

David knew that the repressive atmosphere at Boalt Hall would make many students hesitant to express their views. He therefore wrote in his call for essays that "anonymous submissions will be accepted." Owing to the boldness of the contributors, all of whom rose to their moment in history, of the twenty-seven submissions David received only three authors requested anonymity. Only one of the essays was submitted anonymously. To be sure, all of the contributors understood the potential consequences of publishing views that were demonstrably unwelcome on their campus. But this is precisely why they chose to protect their right, and the right of those who come after them, to free speech. A number of the writers here appear reluctant to speak out, but the urgency of their convictions won the day.

What these UC Berkeley law school students have to say is extremely important. Indeed, their very willingness to publish their essays speaks volumes. The state of democracy in America has much to do with what the country's law schools are teaching a new generation of American lawyers.

Our country is based on justice grounded in the possibility of a fair, free, reasonable pursuit of truth. Anyone with an interest in the American justice system, higher education, intellectual freedom, free speech, and a number of other important issues will read the essays that follow with considerable interest. It is my hope you will read with an open mind and with an eye to reflection. The issues broached and treated in these essays are complex. If this book causes its readers to consider them further, it will have achieved its goal: widening the perspective on one of the most important issues in American education today. The ramifications of the diversity hoax are enormous. This book should open all of our eyes.

PART ONE: The History

The History

By David Wienir, Boalt Hall Class of 2000

The institutional practice of racial preference is just about over in California, and some people are upset – very upset. California's Proposition 209, which banned government-sponsored racial discrimination, including racial preference in admissions decisions at University of California campuses, turned the University of California, Berkeley School of Law (Boalt Hall) into ground zero for the affirmative action debate. The fabric of the entering class changed noticeably from previous years – in the fall of 1997, only one black arrived as a first-year student.

But that number does not tell the whole story. Eighteen black students were accepted to Boalt Hall in 1997, but none chose to attend. The eighteen who gained admission were so qualified that they not only merited acceptance to Berkeley even after Proposition 209; many also gained acceptance to even more prestigious law schools such as Harvard and Yale. The one black student who did attend Boalt as a member of the entering class in 1997 was actually admitted in 1996, while a policy of racial preference was still in place.

Although Proposition 209 merely made academic achievement the absolute criterion for admission to one of the nation's "top-ten" law schools, it had a number of more noticeable effects. Many people at Boalt geared up to turn back the clock. In the classrooms, hallways, bathroom stalls, and bars, students and faculty bemoaned the lack of "diversity" due to the "resegregation" of campus. These fierce opponents of Proposition 209 (and less-than-tolerant enemies of the Californians who supported it) rallied behind the claim that education itself was being compromised by racial homogeneity.

As a result, the Class of 2000 at Boalt Hall School of Law may very well be the most talked about law school class in modern legal history. Boalt has become a flash point for the struggle over racial preferences and the struggle for ethnic diversity. One of the greatest fears expressed by opponents of Proposition 209 is that, despite raising the academic qualifications of the admitted class, the lack of ethnic diversity will compromise the quality of education received at the law school.

Marjorie Shultz, a Boalt professor and 1976 Boalt graduate, exclaimed: "how can [they] be excellent collectively if [they] have experiences that are narrower than the experiences of this population?"[1] The dean of Boalt Hall, Herma Hill Kay, also asserted that without ethnic diversity, "it is more difficult to have a classroom discussion."[2]

It is virtually undeniable that the law school at Berkeley is suffering from a lack of diversity, and that the education at Boalt has indeed been compromised. Any diminishment of the quality of education at Boalt Hall has, however, little to do with race. It has everything to do with intellectual freedom.

The Class of 2000 has strongly supported the proposition that race serves as a proxy for opinion – that diversity is compromised only when *certain* ethnic groups are not adequately represented. Joshua Irwin, a fellow member of the Class of 2000, told the Sacramento Bee, "I think that there's not going to be as many views represented in this class."[3]

Can the diversity of views on campus really be equated with skin color? It ought not to be. Under the name of racial diversity, however, it appears that the value of true diversity of opinion is ignored, and free speech is attacked. Blacks, Asians, and Hispanics who espouse

---

[1] *Los Angeles Times*, August 19, 1997, A3.

[2] *Los Angeles Times*, August 19, 1997, A3.

[3] *Sacramento Bee*, August 19, 1997, A4.

conservative views are called ugly names – whites who espouse conservative views are, regardless of all facts, called racists. Diversity is defined according to skin color, rather than according to ideas.

Scare tactics, parading as enlightened "politically correct" peer pressure, are all part of the fight to control the definition of "diversity" at Berkeley. Within the first month of school, certain members of the Class of 2000 authored an open letter, addressed to the dean, for all students of the class to sign. Those who signed the letter confessed that they "chose to attend Boalt in spite of [their] grave disappointment in the lack of diversity evidenced in the Class of 2000." The letter professed that "completely abolishing [racial preferences] without implementing any other sufficient means of achieving diversity has compromised our legal education. The pool of background experiences and perspectives we are exposed to has diminished significantly, limiting our opportunities for intellectual growth."[4] Seventy-one percent of the entering class signed the letter, and there was scarce evidence at Boalt that those among the twenty-nine percent minority were welcome to speak. I myself was one among the palpably silent twenty-nine percent.

A Hypocritical Definition of "Diversity"

Those who signed the letter seemed to see themselves as more empowered and enlightened than their dissenting contemporaries. Those who refused to sign the letter were – I speak from experience – scorned and disparaged. The intolerance of the authors of this open letter was clearly paradoxical: on the one hand, they espoused "diversity"; on the other hand, they rejected anything but groupthink. Support them, in other words, or be prepared for a gross slinging of names that largely stick.

Indeed, given the fact that control of the definition of not only "diversity" but also of "minority" is in the hands of people with a narrow agenda, great harm has come to minorities themselves. At Berkeley, Asian-Americans have actually been considered an "overrepresented" minority. This unfortunate phrase means that the per-

---

[4] *San Francisco Examiner*, Sept 13, 1997, A3.

centage of Asian-Americans admitted to Berkeley is higher than the percentage of Asian-Americans in the population. As a result, before Proposition 209, Asian-Americans were discriminated against; Berkeley didn't always accept as many as deserved to be accepted because they would have filled places reserved for "under-represented" minorities. In short, under a policy of racial prefer-ences, some poor, hardworking, and deserving minority applicants were being discriminated against in the interest of preferring other minority applicants who were academically less qualified. The les-son to the "over-represented" minorities: achieve and be punished. The lesson to "under-represented" minorities: if you don't achieve, demand to be rewarded on racial grounds.

In the spirit of Dr. Martin Luther King, Jr., I do not believe that the color of one's skin dictates the content of one's character – or opinions. Hence, I do not believe that education at Berkeley is nec-essarily being compromised by the decline in the number of African-Americans in the Class of 2000. I would like to see more black students studying at Boalt Hall as soon as possible, but I must also assert the right of all more qualified students – be they Asian, Hispanic, or even white – to compete on a level playing field. I believe it is neither legal nor moral to offer certain protection to some ethnic groups and not to others.

My beliefs, however, much like Dr. King's beliefs, don't really count nowadays. Nor does the clear language of the 1964 Civil Rights Act, which outlawed racial discrimination, and on which Proposition 209 was based. My decision not to sign the open letter to the dean resulted in unfounded allegations that I was a racist. The underlying assumption (a tawdry tactic we'd hate to see in a court of law) is that anyone who does not support racial preferences is a racist at heart.

At Boalt, each entering class is arbitrarily divided by the admin-istration into modules. I was in module seven. For some reason, module seven was comprised of a large percentage of students who did not wish to sign the petition. This uncommonly high percentage in one module was unacceptable to many students comprising the seventy-one percent majority. As a result, within the first month of school, my module became popularly known as "Satan Seven."

Early on, it became clear that my dissenting opinions on such issues as racial preferences frustrated those students who passionately sought to create a racially engineered society without diversity of thought. In my first year of law school, rather than finding myself sitting at a round table of legal discussion, I discovered that I was immersed in a sea of intolerance.

Many Boalt students act as if their education is threatened whenever any conservative view is expressed. One conservative opinion per class is more than they can stand. Ironically, the conservative views are generally those supporting liberal notions of freedom of expression. Still, almost every time a lone conservative tried to raise his or her voice during my first year at Boalt, things got ugly. Fists, rather than hands, were raised. Eyes rolled. Glares flashed. Intolerance radiated. Diversity of mind was declared dangerous and unwanted. Only racial diversity was celebrated and cherished.

In Boalt's law library, there exists a public journal where students are free to write in questions and comments. The questions are addressed to an anonymous figure called "Uncle Zeb," who responds to the worries of the Boalt community. Students are free to flip through the pages and become aware of the concerns of their fellow classmates. I remember reading one question in particular. A student was thinking about dropping out of law school – the student suggested that he or she was not able to tolerate hearing conservative ideas in a Berkeley classroom.

Imagine. No, don't imagine. Understand. This is a future lawyer unable even to listen to a dissenting opinion – unable to protect the very liberal principle of tolerance upon which America was founded.

This narrow-mindedness is perpetuated not only by a large number of students, but by faculty and administrators as well. It appears to be institutionalized. At the time this book was conceived, one of the most important people in California was Governor Pete Wilson, a Boalt Hall graduate. Although portraits of other alumni were scattered throughout the law school complex, nowhere was there a portrait of Wilson. When I approached a dean and asked why the Governor of California was not pictorially represented, the dean responded by saying that Wilson was not one of Boalt's finest students. She said that he was not very active while a student. I believe the message I received was clear: Wilson's views do not "represent" Boalt Hall.

During my first year of law school at Boalt, I began to understand the methods of the radical Left to be nothing short of intellectual terrorism. Unable to accomplish their goals through ordinary means in a democratic society (i.e., a California initiative), they have resorted to other methods to enforce their will. Many of the essays that follow chronicle their tactics.

The intolerant activists, comprised of both Boalt students and other enthusiasts, have personally attacked students who express contrary views by using techniques of slander, intimidation, and pejorative personal statements. They have torn down flyers of organizations with diverse views. They have marched up and down the halls chanting militant slogans such as "Let them in or tear it down" ("them" referring to under-qualified minority students who had not gained admission under the new race-blind admission policies, "it" referring to the university). They have interrupted classes by insulting professors, blowing whistles, and screaming into loudspeakers. They have singled out white students (or students they assumed, sometimes wrongly, to be white) and strongly suggested that they give up their seats to minority students whom the protesters had imported. The campus has been defaced. Fire alarms have been pulled. Many of the students even came to class in full uniform, wearing identical T-shirts signifying their desire to ethnically reengineer the law school. The language that the 'diversity' protesters used was clear. On the walls they wrote: "FUCK 209" and "SUPPORT DIVERSITY, NOT BOALT."

What is most alarming is the kind of balkanizing separatism they seek to effect in America. They are at war with American values of meritocracy, freedom of thought, and open intellectual discourse. This behavior is boorish, immature, and unacceptable in an institution that should be devoted to free and open discussion of ideas. At places such as Berkeley, polite disagreement is too frequently shunned as a rational method of the West that defeats the pressing goal of overturning Proposition 209. The unwillingness of law students merely to listen to the other side of an argument is frightening.

Berkeley Is Not Unique

While this book was written about Boalt, it would be incorrect to assume that the problems it describes are unique to its halls. The scope of this book is much greater than the uncivil actions of a small number of Berkeley radicals. If only we could be so lucky. If only the disease of contemptuous intolerance were so well contained. Berkeley serves as the perfect backdrop for the first comprehensive collection of essays published by students dealing with the loss of intellectual freedom within a "top ten" law school. What is particularly troubling is that so many law students seem to be sanctioning an attack upon reason itself, upon the foundation of justice and objectivity upon which America is based.

Much has already been written on the nationwide threats of "illiberal education,"[5] the "tempting of America,"[6] and "the radical assault on truth in American law."[7] These works have illuminated many readers.

Most recently, Daniel Farber and Suzanna Sherry, in *Beyond All Reason*, directly address the concerns of intellectual diversity in law school. Writing from the law school of the University of Minnesota in 1997, these two professors were brave enough to document "the paranoid mode of thought in American legal theory" that has intellectually paralyzed many law schools. They remark that challenges to liberal ideas "are often rejected as not merely incorrect but illegitimate, symptomatic of racism and sexism and therefore not worthy of serious intellectual engagement."[8] Among the many examples the authors provide, particularly telling is former Harvard law professor "Derrick Bell's assertion that critiques of critical race theory should

---

[5] Dinesh D'Souza, *Illiberal Education* (New York: The Free Press, 1991).

[6] Robert Bork, *The Tempting of America*, (New York: The Free Press, 1990).

[7] Daniel A. Farber and Suzanna Sherry, *Beyond All Reason: The Radical Assault on Truth in American Law*, (Oxford: Oxford University Press, 1997).

[8] *Beyond All Reason*, 134.

not be dignified with a response."[9] Bell's contemptuous refusal to debate should have no place in the training of lawyers. But it does.

Farber and Sherry explain that "radical multiculturalism has a built-in tendency toward just this kind of reaction because of its obsession with power." They note that this quest for power "is not apparent on the surface of things. The metaphors of concealment and deception, which are so characteristic of radical multicultural-ism, tell how the iron hand of power is hidden within the velvet glove of 'neutral principles.'"[10] The result is a "threat to efforts at dialogue between radical multiculturalists and others," and "it makes genuine intellectual engagement with outsiders difficult."[11]

The attack upon civil discussion in law school classes has dire consequences. But students rarely speak of such issues. Those who need to be heard have largely remained silent.

Un-Silencing the Minority

At Berkeley, my voice was not supposed to be heard. I was supposed to count only as one of those hateful, oppressive opponents of diver-sity. Hidden amidst the shadows of the debate over racial preference, I nevertheless refused to go without putting my ear to what I hoped was fertile ground.

I undertook the task of forwarding a series of questions to the entire student body. Like many of my fellow classmates, I was inter-ested in the question of intellectual diversity, not just racial character-istics. I sent out a call for papers to begin a project I conceived as *The Berkeley Federalist Law Papers*.[12] Accordingly, I asked: "How healthy is the marketplace of ideas at Boalt? Do you have a fair opportunity to share your ideas in the classroom? Does expression flow freely in an environment tolerant of diversity, or does the climate of tolerance at

---

[9] *Beyond All Reason*, 134.

[10] *Beyond All Reason*, 135.

[11] *Beyond All Reason*, 137.

[12] At the time I sent out my call for papers in the fall of 1997, I was a member of the Berkeley Federalist Society. In spring 1998, I was voted Vice President. See "The Question," reprinted below. For a description of the Federalist Society, see Appendix B.

Berkeley paradoxically inhibit true diversity of opinion?"

Provocative questions, no? Still, in the month following the announcement, I received no response. Zero. At first, I was relieved, likely on account of my wish to believe that all was well. But slowly my feelings of relief turned properly to concern.

In 1995, Brian Mass, the former president of the Boalt Hall chapter of The Federalist Society, remarked to the *San Francisco Examiner*: "the emotional climate [at Boalt] is such that anyone trying to defend free speech rights . . . would be called a racist. For someone to take a stand like that, the social pressures are enormous."[13] Now, in 1998, I wondered if students had grown so accustomed to repressing their beliefs that they simply had grown incapable of expressing themselves? Had self-esteem been completely sacrificed for self-denial?

No, not completely. Eventually, students began to write. My personal experiences and concerns regarding the suppression of thought and ideas at Boalt Hall were, submission by submission, loudly confirmed by the words of my fellow students.

This book is a compilation of those student essays, thoughts, and intellectual prayers. According to the student testimonies published here, their opinions and viewpoints have been purposely drowned, held hostage, and repressed at the University of California's premier law school. The very people who have so fervently and sincerely proclaimed themselves to be the greatest defenders of "diversity" were the ones responsible for silencing the voices of concerned students struggling to address the complexities of profound issues.

This book is dedicated to diversity – diversity of thought, and diversity of opinion. It asserts the value of minorities themselves freely to debate diverse opinions. It is dedicated to the belief that all views, if honestly maintained, should receive a proper forum for expression. This is particularly true in America's institutions of higher learning – and especially at law schools. It is unfortunate and ironic that those who earnestly identify themselves as the great defenders of "diversity" are too often the last in line to stand up to defend their

---

[13] *San Francisco Examiner*, March 14, 1995, A15.

fellow students' rights to free expression.

What's worst of all? They, like Professor Bell, appear to be proud of their unwillingness to listen to others. This sad fact is a sign of our times. At colleges around the country, professors indulge themselves and their students by considering only their own political concerns, acting as if the concerns, thoughts, and achievements of others – not only bold conservative minorities of the present but also venerable liberals of the past – are irrelevant. One of the easiest ways to change the present, after all, is to obliterate the past.

The Past Matters: Liberty Comes Hard

The problems we face today are not unique. Hence, valuable insight can and must be learned from the great thinkers of the past. Not only do they provide perspective, but they also offer a conceptual framework upon which to build and a starting point from which to proceed. Without common education in courses that consider the rich Western tradition of intellectual debate, students cannot learn successfully to engage each other in clear, civil debate. What's more, they cannot even listen to each other with comprehension and tolerance. As half-baked anti-Western and anti-American sentiments replace great books in college and university classrooms around the country, more and more students can proudly declare that they refuse to listen to people who disagree with them. We ought to stop and take stock. When students at an elite American law school can state unabashedly their unwillingness to listen to opposing views, it is clear that their legal education is in jeopardy, as is the current and future state of our union.

Lessons taught in the past often need to be relearned in the present. There is very little in life that is new. From one generation to another, we all deal with the same fears, pains, anxieties, and struggles. Today's "liberal" students have much to learn from yesterday's liberals. We as a society still have a lot to learn from the great liberal thinker John Stuart Mill – despite the fact that he is a dead white male. To Mill, freedom of thought and expression was of utmost importance. "If all mankind minus one were of one opinion, and only one person were of the contrary opinion," Mill writes, "mankind would be no more justified in silencing that one person, than he, if he had the power, would be justified in silencing mankind." Mill explains: "To refuse a hearing to an opinion, because they are sure that it is false, is to assume that *their* certainty is the same thing as absolute certainty. All silencing of discussion is an assumption of infallibility."[14]

The specific concern of diversity was important even in the nineteenth century. As Mill writes, "only through diversity of opinion is there, in the existing state of human intellect, a chance of fair play to all sides of the truth. Where there are persons to be found who form an exception to the apparent unanimity of the world on any subject, even if the world is in the right, it is always probable that dissentients have something worth hearing to say for themselves, and that truth would lose something by their silence."[15]

Thought-police and "political correctness" would have seemed more than inappropriate to Mill. Furthermore, the concept of racial and gender diversity would have seemed peculiar. Does an African-American need to be present to argue an African-American point of view? Does a woman need to be present to argue women's point of view? To my knowledge, Mill never spoke directly to this issue. However, it should be noted that to this day, John Stuart Mill, a dead white male, undeniably serves as one of the greatest advocates of women's rights the world has ever known.

To fight for liberty requires selfless conviction. Unfortunately, for feel-good "liberals" today – especially students – pandering and partying too frequently take the place of selfless devotion to the principles of liberty. Recently, while delivering a speech to University of California at San Diego, President Clinton declared "Look around this crowd today. Don't you think you have learned a whole lot more than you would have if everybody sitting around you looked just like you?"[16]

---

[14] John Stuart Mill, *On Liberty*, ed. David Spits (New York: Norton, 1975) 18.

[15] *On Liberty*, 46.

[16] *The San Francisco Chronicle*, June 17,1997, A21.

This confusion of diversity of skin color for diversity of opinion is at the root of a lot of shortsightedness on racial issues. Here's a question: would a young black man learn more by sitting next to Bill Clinton and Al Gore, or by sitting next to Ward Connerly and Jesse Jackson? Of course, opponents of Proposition 209 wouldn't even want to sit near Ward Connerly – and this is the real problem at Berkeley, the real center of the diversity hoax. Now here's another question: would a young white woman learn more by sitting next to Elizabeth Dole and Hillary Clinton, or by sitting next to Bill Clinton and Vernon Jordan. Who knows? You must experience the company of individuals, and combinations of individuals. You must encounter their ideas – and the complex relations between their ideas. You cannot reduce the matter to ethnicity or gender.

The definition of "diversity" is a complex issue, and reducing it to skin color is a form of racism that ignores the diversity of opinions not only among populations, but among minorities themselves.

If he had the chance, Mill would not likely have contributed to President Clinton's campaign, nor espoused his views on racial preference. If alive today, Mill would be likely to celebrate Brian W. Jones, the former president of the Center for New Black Leadership in Washington, D.C. "Our emphasis on race today," Jones writes, "in no way assures us of the intellectual diversity we seek...To achieve the multiplicity of viewpoints that facilitates the search for truth, our diversity efforts must focus upon genuine intellectual diversity."[17] Jones explains: "no two human beings can ever be expected to have a preordained viewpoint or perspective, based simply or even largely upon the mere experience of being an American of a particular race. It is the uniqueness of the human spirit that animates the perspective each of us brings to the world around us. The color of my skin simply says nothing about the content of my mind and character."[18]

At Boalt Hall, the uniqueness of the human spirit is, to many, mere fantasy. They see any attempt to argue for its validity as unacceptable. People do not exist in themselves, but live only through

---

[17] Brian W. Jones, "The Meaning of Diversity," *Philanthropy*, Fall 1996, 5.

[18] "The Meaning of Diversity," 7.

racial, gender, and class associations – or so undergraduates are persuaded to think at so many of America's colleges and universities. This is the basic assumption adhered to by many at Boalt. This is the essential justification for silencing opposing perspectives and promoting a totalitarian "politically correct" homogeneity. Diversity of skin color – at least for certain "preferred minorities" – is everything. Diversity of viewpoints, in contrast, is an oppressive burden.

The Dangers of Denial

Regardless of race, class, or gender, we all have one choice in the face of any fact: to accept it or to evade it. Many at Boalt Hall have done the latter. In the parable "The Emperor's New Clothes," anyone who failed to perceive the Emperor's fine garments was considered depraved and evil, even though those garments did not exist. At Boalt today, many students and faculty profess admiration for nonexistent intellectual diversity and freedom. It is an accepted belief that anyone who fails to perceive such freedom is in error.

Before we can solve any problem, it must first be accepted that a problem in fact exists. Boalt, however, stuck in a semi-conscious daze, has been so focused on racial diversity that the importance of diversity of ideas has been all but forgotten. University of California Regent Ward Connerly has correctly noted that "the notion of using race to achieve diversity is so deeply embedded in [Dean Kay] that she's not conscious of the negative effect she is having."[19]

Indeed, many academics are completely unwilling (or unable) to realize that a problem exists at Boalt. At the end of each semester, many of my professors, as if reading from a prepared statement, expressed thanks for the wide range of ideas and perspectives that were offered during the semester. I sat amazed – it was as if they were pouring salt onto the wounds of all those who had been effectively silenced.

The administration's unwillingness to address this issue is well documented. In a 1995 Wall Street Journal Op-Ed article entitled "Why I hate the 'D' Word," Matthew Covington, then a prospective

---

[19] *San Francisco Examiner*, July 27, 1997, A1.

student, recounted his disheartening experience at a 1995 spring visit day for admitted students. It would have been enough that he was not invited to have lunch with any "student organization" because he had white skin. However, during the pre-orientation program, Mr. Covington recalls that an imposing black alumna "delivered a militant tirade against the current civil rights initiative in California to curtail racially based preferences in hiring and admissions. She circulated petitions for us to sign," he writes, "and exhorted us to resist the 'war against people of color.' She said little about the law school save that she had hated her experience there. When the tirade finally ended," Covington writes, "the law students' president, moderating the panel, explained, 'I think we're ready to take to the streets.' What an odd recourse for aspiring lawyers."[20]

Aspiring lawyers ought to be dedicated to freedom of speech, which guarantees true diversity. Mr. Covington concluded by observing that, at Boalt, this "sacred diversity was not evident. Presumably there are heterosexual white men in the school, but none were on the panel. And certainly there was no diversity of ideology. That reasonable people can be opposed to race-based quotas was not even considered."[21]

A few weeks later, Herma Hill Kay, the dean of Boalt Hall, wrote a letter to the editor in response to Mr. Covington's Op-Ed piece. She boldly stated: "I would like to assure Mr. Covington that his experience is not typical of life at Boalt and that both his views and his willingness to express them are welcome here."[22]

Many students who submitted their essays to me, self-described liberal democrats among them, clearly agree with Mr. Covington. We are faced with a crisis few are brave enough to address. The marketplace of ideas at Boalt is not open to anyone who wants to think, but is open only to individuals who want to think in a certain way. After witnessing such a spectacle, Mr. Covington chose not to attend law school at Boalt Hall. When he rejected Boalt's offer of admission,

---

[20] *Wall Street Journal*, May 12, 1995, A12.

[21] *Wall Street Journal*, May 12, 1995, A12

[22] "Don't Judge Boalt on One Bad Day," *Wall Street Journal*, June 6, 1995, A19.

Mr. Covington perhaps had in mind Goya's famous *The Sleep of Reason Produces Monsters.*

Why this Book

One inauspicious, late night at the law school, I encountered a professor. I was, doubtless, visibly upset. Why was I upset? I had just attended what was to be an open forum discussion on racial preference that quickly turned into a conservative witch-hunt. In championing ethnic diversity, the students who favored racial preferences loudly scorned all forms of individual achievement; they perceived no difference between earned and unearned rewards. They sought to enshrine mediocrity. They claimed that the LSAT was biased against minorities and the poor.

Basically, they seemed to despise whatever seemed to frustrate their attempts to reconstruct social reality into a "feel good" egalitarianism – that is, not equality of opportunity but equality of outcome. Objective truth and morality, they seemed to imply, were just a manifestation of white hegemony. As intolerant and irrational as these students were, their attack was having an effect upon me. I cannot imagine any person could face such fierce intolerance unscathed.

I approached the professor, who had been at Boalt for a long time. I was so upset that I started to ask questions to which I, by then, knew the answers: Does anyone take these students seriously? The professor responded calmly. The answer was yes. Do they have any lasting effect on administrative policy within the law school? Again, the professor responded calmly. Again, the answer was yes. I recall sighing. But doesn't every administrator realize that some of these students are merely bullies, and that a very large number of good-hearted, reasonable students disagree with them? The professor responded, still calmly. Now the answer was no. At that moment, the importance of this project became clear.

This book is intended to create a moment of pause and reflection. This book is not written by academics, professors, or politicians. There is no secret agenda. It is written by UC Berkeley law students. My goal is for a copy of this book to sit on the desk of every dean, academic, and student in the nation. This book allows the world to see what many students see – and feel what they feel. I hope it will make people think. I hope it will help people to realize that there is a problem, and address it.

This book lets those who are actually affected by intolerance in academia speak for themselves; they capture a world that is so concealed that even professors in the classroom are often left unaware. The essays are personal and compelling. They represent individual students' perceptions of the environment in which they learn. They are snapshots into the minds of students studying amidst paradoxes, unfounded allegations, and restrictions and limitations of free thought and ideas. They should be taken seriously.

The Contributors

The students who contributed to this volume are truly courageous. They are willing to think and express themselves in what is a repressive environment. They are people who value freedom of thought. They are people who are not willing to abandon their values and ideas. They are, rather, eager to test their thoughts by subjecting them to free and open discourse. It is for this reason that many of these students came to Boalt Hall. Seeing that intellectual freedom is stifled at Boalt, these students have dared to take the first step toward freedom. They have realized that complacency means surrender, and that surrender means self-destruction. They have realized the primacy of ideas and the need to share them. I am grateful to each and every contributor.

Each essay is subjective and speaks only for itself. Each contributor relates the facts as he or she perceived them. Each essay was submitted blindly, without any opportunity to review the work of others. This was not a group project. This collection records the observations of concerned individual students, some of whom know each other, some of whom know neither each other nor me. Of the twenty-seven essays submitted, two disagree with the notion that there is a problem with respect to intellectual diversity and freedom. In the interest of truth and freedom of expression, no submissions have been omitted. Every student who cared enough to submit his or her view on the topic has been published here. Each writer thought independently, yet for the most part the voices speak as a unified whole. The message is plain – there is a problem that needs to be addressed.

There are more than 700 students at Boalt Hall and only twenty-seven essays here. This collection therefore makes no claim to speak on behalf of the entire student body or of Boalt Hall itself. These essays represent the view of a minority of students at Boalt Hall. The real question here is the size of the minority for which the contributors speak. Only a small portion of the daily readers of the *New York Times* ever writes a letter to the editor. But for every person who does write, there are many who agree with the points expressed but who, for whatever reason, choose not to air their opinions in a public forum. Given the nature of this book, fear of reprisal was one reason not to contribute, as a number of would-be contributors told me in response to my call for papers. In a less intolerant atmosphere, I might have been deluged with essays. But in a more tolerant atmosphere, there would have been no need – and no subject – for such a book at all.

All contributors were actively studying at Boalt Hall during the academic year 1997-98, the time when all but one of these essays were written. Some contributors were in their twenties, some were in their forties. Men and women contributed. Some had blond hair, while others had brown or red hair. Many of the contributors were considered "minorities" when they applied to the law school. To my knowledge the contributors are racially diverse. East Asians, Near-East Asians, Hispanics, and others of various religious and ethnic backgrounds contributed to this publication. As I fervently believe that diversity of opinion has little if anything to do with gender, race, or hair color, such information about each writer is not specified. I received twenty-seven essays. All of them are printed here. While some essays needed minor grammatical and stylistic corrections, most are published largely untouched. Only three contributors asked to be anonymous. Only one essay was submitted anonymously. The effort and resolve of those who contributed to this volume ought to be celebrated.

The timely participation of the contributors demonstrates the sense of urgency expressed in this book. Many students wrote their essays while studying for "all-important" law school exams. One student submitted his essay less than 48 hours before he was due to be married. Another student actually broke down into tears when she discussed submitting her essay. No student received any form of monetary compensation for his or her contribution. For the most part, it was not even clear if the project, *The Berkeley Federalist Law Papers*, would even be published. To my knowledge, only about a quarter of the contributors were active members of the Berkeley Federalist Society, a fact which speaks to the desire of the contributors to address an important problem. The writing is pure, heartfelt, and immediate, but also reasoned.

To my knowledge, no book had ever been published by a collection of concerned law students commenting on the intellectual health of their institution. Lawyers always look to precedent, and we had none to follow. Lawyers are trained to be cautious and seldom to commit – these future lawyers were willing to make bold and important statements.

Historically, what has made Berkeley an outstanding academic institution is not only its willingness to question, but also the eagerness of its students to respond. This is no less true today than at any time in the past. I posed a question. The students bravely responded. For this reason alone, I am grateful to have been accepted to Boalt and would enthusiastically encourage all accepted students to attend. Even conservatives. The reader should not think for a moment that this project has been driven by bitterness or scorn. Rather, this book has been inspired by unbridled optimism and hope for change. The future is bright – but requires thought and action by those who care.

The cathartic effect that this book has had on the students who contributed appears to have been profound. Through writing for this publication, many students told me that, for the first time, they were able to formulate and organize their perceptions. I hope that students across the nation who are concerned with open and free debate and intellectual honesty will realize that they are not alone. I hope that readers will become less tolerant of intolerance, and will realize the consequences of remaining silent and not making their world a better place.

This said, I must voice one regret – that we didn't have even more contributors. Many students approached me throughout the writing of this book, and expressed their regret for not being brave enough to contribute. They told me that I was risking my career and reputation in the legal profession. The consequences of such a project, they said, might be adverse. So be it. Ideas will outlive any one man. Ideas mold the world in which we live – they are not mere abstractions. One must struggle for one's convictions.

On a Personal Note

I shall end with one final, hopeful recollection. Every first-year law student at Boalt is asked to participate in a Moot Court competition in the spring semester. After selecting a partner, the next step is choosing the case one wishes to argue. The list of cases covered a wide range of topics: drug testing, state-imposed birth control, affirmative action, and many others. The issue of arguing against affirmative action appeared to be the least desirable to the first-year students. There were many possible reasons why this was the case: students were likely either overwhelmed or intimidated by the topic. At first, like many of my colleagues, my partner and I ranked the issue of affirmative action last on our list of preferences. Later that night, after an open and healthy debate, we decided that we would take the case.

A few weeks later we learned that we had been selected to argue the case against affirmative action. Opposing counsel would include the only African-American in our class. By the end of the competition, we had learned a very valuable lesson: dialogue and debate, even on personal and emotionally charged topics, were possible with civility and respect. The night that we argued the case, my partner and I celebrated. I was hopeful. I still am.

My personal background has led me to care a great deal about this book. I grew up in a moderate, economically conservative family in a Los Angeles suburb. My parents voted for Reagan. My old high school nemesis, whom I greatly respect, is currently the president of the Sierra Club. I did not cry when Jerry Garcia died. I clearly identify myself as a moderate Republican. Still, I have always been a person who seeks to learn from diverse people with opposing views. Indeed, while earning my master's degree at the London School of Economics in 1995-1996, I worked for the Labour Party within the House of Commons. Immediately before attending Boalt, I worked for the Survivors of the Shoah Visual History Foundation, a non-profit foundation dedicated to promoting ethnic tolerance and understanding.

What excited me most about attending law school at UC Berkeley was its legacy of being an intellectually free university. I presumed Boalt Hall would be the ideal place to expose myself to a true diversity of perspectives. I was horrified at what I discovered. I was angered that, in seeking truth, I was denied an encouraging environment in which to explore my views.

Many Latino students at Boalt proclaim themselves to be the sole representative of their people, and many women appoint themselves as the solitary voice for women everywhere, and many gay students crown themselves ambassadors of all gay interests. I do not view myself as representative of any group. But those who embrace group-think and "identity politics" do. Hence, I was viewed as the manifestation of all that is white, heterosexual, and evil. In an irrational display of racism and bigotry, I was declared the enemy. As everybody knows that there is nothing to gain by chatting with the devil, dialogue was closed. Despite being accepted to Boalt, it appeared to me that the law school did not want me around – so I made myself as scarce as possible. This was difficult, however, since I lived directly across the street.

I came to Berkeley sympathetic to some of the issues of the liberal Democratic agenda, and remain so. However, I am adamant that the tactics of the intolerant radical activists actually erode the validity of much that they have to say. As I gazed across the historic campus late one April night, I wondered whatever happened to the Berkeley of the sixties – a Berkeley that celebrated freedom of expression, and despised narrow-mindedness.

The 1997-98 academic year was full of turmoil. There were many moments when I felt awful. On one occasion in particular, perhaps the worst day of all the protests, I spoke at length with Dean

Kay in a hallway regarding the very issues this book addresses. Standing with my dean, I was in the midst of a breakdown of order as the protesters brought the law school to an anarchic standstill. Throughout that day, Dean Kay was verbally attacked. It was a trying day for all reasonable people with good intentions at Boalt.

It must be emphasized that no specific individuals are to be blamed. No administrators are particularly at fault. I have discussed my plans for this book with the deans of the law school, and they have been very encouraging. They told me that they looked forward to reading the collected essays, and I believe they were sincere. One thing that disturbed me most was to see the disrespect afforded to the deans. I believe that Dean Kay, and other deans as well, will be curious to read about the experiences of the students at their school – for indeed, we are all in this together. Like many students, Dean Kay herself was attacked. I was ashamed by the treatment Dean Kay and her colleagues received from the 'diversity' protesters throughout the year. The administration has my great respect, as do my classmates who struggle for truly liberal, open, free interchange of ideas. The 'diversity' protesters treated Dean Kay horribly, and this treatment was part of a larger hypocrisy at the root of their tactics. As Heather McCormick writes, "While I endorse efforts to increase minority enrollment at Boalt, there was no way I was going to stand in the Dean's office and shout down a woman who has devoted a lifetime to defending the rights of women and minorities."

The 'diversity' protesters did much to destroy the Boalt Hall community. Perhaps the worst consequence was that as free speech and open debate were threatened, people did not find themselves in an atmosphere conducive to bringing workable solutions to real problems. I hope that the observations in this book will make people of all opinions engage in – and support the value of – free and open intellectual debate.

THE QUESTION

The call for papers, which is printed below, was sent out to every student in the Boalt community. For most contributors, this was all the students saw before deciding either to contribute or to ignore the project. A few contributors contacted David Wienir for further information. In most cases, the essays were submitted many months later, after people had time to reflect upon their experiences at Boalt. The book was initially entitled The Berkeley Federalist Law Papers. *Upon final revision for publication, based on the general message of the contributions, the title was changed to its current form.*

TO ALL BOALT STUDENTS
HEY, THIS MEANS YOU!

THE BERKELEY FEDERALIST LAW PAPERS is dedicated to broadening intellectual debate among students and members of the legal community. As a nonpartisan publication, its objective is to stimulate scholarly discourse by providing a forum for open and honest expression.

The first issue, to be published this spring, will consist of student submissions. The theme is simple yet poignant. How healthy is the marketplace of ideas here at Boalt? Do you have fair opportunity to share your ideas in the classroom? Does expression flow freely in an environment tolerant of diversity, or does the climate of tolerance at Berkeley paradoxically inhibit true diversity of opinion? Has political activism within the classroom silenced important student perspectives? What should have been said, but never was? Finally, here is an opportunity to speak.

Seeking "diary-like" submissions, The Papers is interested in candid opinions about your law school experience. All viewpoints are welcome and encouraged. There are no length requirements. Anything more than a sentence and less than 3 pages will be sufficient.

Example #1: Boalt is very healthy. Conservatives and liberals are equally free to express their opinions. I can remember the time when...

Example #2: I never talk in class anymore. It just is not worth it. The one time I did, I was labeled an enemy of the people. It was awful. All I said was...

What has been your experience at Boalt? Let your voice be heard. A little can say a lot. Just an hour of your time can make an enormous difference. I beg you all to take full advantage of this unique opportunity. Anonymous submissions will be accepted.

Sincerely,

David Wienir
Editor-in-Chief

PART TWO: The Voices

CHAPTER ONE

THE IDEA OF DIVERSITY

There is nothing more important to consider deeply and freely than the idea of diversity. As the three essays in this brief chapter relate, to these students few things have been more disturbing during their time at UC Berkeley than the encroachments upon the freedom to investigate ideas diversely – especially the idea of diversity itself.

Losing the King's Peace
By Richard MacBride

In the Middle Ages in England, one of the punishments which could be meted out to criminals was to "lose the king's peace." This meant that the civil authorities would no longer protect the criminal's physical well-being – any person who found the criminal was free to kill him with impunity. Only certain crimes were considered serious enough to warrant re-classifying the criminal as an outcast in this way.

In the marketplace of ideas in American society, there have always been ideas which placed the believers in a pariah category similar to losing the king's peace; the general populace feels free to scorn the holders of these ideas as crazy, stupid, and dangerous. Serious discussion of the offending ideas is not admitted, since "everyone" agrees that the ideas are without merit. Over time, the unacceptable ideas in America have changed. For example, in the 1950's, being labeled a communist was sometimes enough to "lose the king's peace" in American society, i.e., lose one's job, passport, and friends. Nowadays, by contrast, one can walk down the street with an armful of Marx's *Communist Manifesto* and few people would care.

I write these few rambling words because I have noticed that at Boalt, a place where I would hope to find a more tolerant marketplace of ideas than in the society at large, it can be easy to lose the king's peace and quickly come to be regarded as a fool or worse. Several topics of recent import have caught my attention in this regard. For example, the topics of affirmative action, immigration reform, and welfare reform have provoked serious debate at the state and national levels; it appears that the national dialogue as a whole finds merit in considering a number of different angles on these topics. I have not heard of any leaders from any part of the political spectrum say that we need to leave the situation exactly as it is on these topics, or that everything is working just fine. On the contrary, the national dialogue has approached these topics for what they are, extremely complex and nuanced. And yet, at Boalt, it sometimes seems that, if one does not espouse the "one correct" opinion on these and other topics, one is viewed as a fascist or a fool. A worse offense still, it seems, is to try to analyze the "one correct" opinion to see if it has flaws; then one truly risks being labeled "dangerous."

My hope for an institution like Boalt is not that we simply feel comfortable in automatically dismissing people who espouse unpopular views. My hope is rather that such assertions cause us to reflect on the way in which controversial topics can be distorted and manipulated by interested parties for their own ends. For example, we may ask why someone would assert such an idea. What does he or she gain from it? Who does he or she represent? As future lawyers, this is, in my opinion, a much more productive approach to today's controversial topics than simply dismissing "fringe" ideas as the product of evil or mentally ill people. Boalt ought to be a marketplace of ideas and a place where we learn new ways of thinking about our world. Today's unpopular opinions may be tomorrow's truths, or vice versa.

I encourage all Boalt students to move beyond the limited dynamic in which there are two categories of opinions: "correct" opinions, which we need not examine, and "nutcase" opinions, which cause the opinion holder to lose the king's peace and be treated like a fool. The right to free speech should not have to mean being forced to choose between agreeing with a person or risk losing his or her respect. I am surprised that I find myself feeling compelled to write this, but given the institution of political correctness, I will conclude by reminding the reader that different people hold different views on most topics, and people should not be made to feel like fools because they do not hold yours or mine.

The Great Buzzword
By Anthony Patel

Diversity – that is the buzzword which has taken UC Berkeley's School of Law by storm throughout the 1997-98 academic year. Proponents of diversity at Boalt have pressed for everything from a diversity of race, ethnicity, gender, and sexual orientation. The study of law and legal institutions at Boalt has been trumped by issues of affirmative action, race, and politics.

I understand that both the law and law schools are not insulated (nor should they be) from politics and current events. But it is my belief that the people of the state of California created Boalt Hall for the study of law, not for the disruptive practices (i.e., walk-outs, walk-ins, sit-ins, sit-outs, etc.) that radicals at Boalt have espoused to make their points about diversity and affirmative action.

The discussion about diversity and race has done nothing at Boalt except to suppress the free flow of ideas and thoughts. In my experience, the liberals have dominated class discussions and debate here at Boalt to such an extent that very little diversity of ideas exists in reality. Conservative, even moderate students, who disagree with the vociferous supporters of diversity are reluctant to speak in class for fear of being bombarded by insults and poignant barbs from radical students. It is ironic that the very movement that was supposed to promote diversity and an exchange of differences has done nothing but the opposite – quell free expression and debate at Boalt. It is my contention that there is little discussion or debate at Boalt about diversity – it is accepted blindly as "a good," and anyone who disagrees is discouraged from speaking out.

The funny thing is that I came to Boalt expecting the worst. I was prepared to meet a group of left-wing liberals who would disagree with everything that I had to say. And I did. But, for the most part, students at Boalt are willing to tolerate other views and political philosophies. Most of my fellow students are perfectly tolerant of conservative views and differences of opinions. Unfortunately, a very small group of students who are unwilling to allow free debate to flourish have seized the agenda at Boalt. Most of the discussions in class and in the hallways of the law school have been dominated by this small contingent of students. In my opinion, they have ruined a large part of the law school experience (exchanging different ideas with your colleagues) for many of us.

In the coming years, I hope that the discussion and crusade for diversity turns to factors other than racial and gender composition. I have never been a fan of either "diversity" or the values that it promotes, but if we are going to be committed to ensuring some sort of diverse student body at Boalt, we should try to ensure that intellectual and ideological diversity are just as important as race and gender. In the end, I hope that all the hoorah and impetus behind the diversity movement die down, and that we can go back to studying the law at Boalt Hall – as our predecessors once did.

Boalt is No Exception

*Anonymous**

Human nature is often similar across ideological, racial, religious, and gender lines. One trait humans have in common is a tendency to suppress views not in agreement with their own, if possible. Of course, a minority will push for open channels until they become a majority or achieve a position of power. UC Berkeley School of Law is not an exception to this generalization.

I have found there is a vocal group of students who make it difficult for me to honestly express my more conservative views. It isn't that I'm even all that conservative. Any conservative worth her salt would label me a liberal. Statements, which appear to be "politically correct," often get jumped on by a group of a few students who know the truth and don't wish to be bothered by the facts.

What bothers me most is the inability to have a dialogue with other students at Boalt unless they already think the same way as I do. This may be because of the highly charged and emotional nature of affirmative action and racial injustice. If all sides were willing to allow the open and honest expression of thoughts and ideas, we just might be surprised at what we could learn from each other.

---

* *Editors' Note:* The fact that the person who submitted this piece agreed to publish it only on the condition that it be published anonymously speaks as loudly as the concerns raised. The contributor expressed concern about any possible consequences that might arise from attaching

his or her name to his or her view. Given the civil (even innocuous) tone of this essay, the author's decision to publish anonymously serves as a testament to the pressures of the intellectual climate at Berkeley and the bravery of all of the contributors who publish their views herein.

CHAPTER TWO

THE LACK OF DIALOGUE

Nothing is more essential to education than dialogue – especially among students who do not agree. Not only does dialogue need to occur; once it does, students need to listen, and listen well, with a willingness to understand and to debate more rigorously.

The Unprofitable Monopoly
By Heather McCormick

I came to Boalt Hall with the optimism shared by many first-year students. If ever there were a place where open-minded people would engage in dialogue and emerge for the better, it would be UC Berkeley School of Law (Boalt Hall). Four years later, I no longer share that optimism. For I have found that the "marketplace of ideas" at Boalt is actually a monopoly.

My first big lesson in the silencing of dialogue happened in first-year property class. The professor – thankfully a visiting one – showed a video on housing discrimination. After the video, she called for an open dialogue, encouraging everyone to express what they felt about what they had seen. As the exchange progressed, one of my classmates raised his hand, with a hypothetical based on reverse discrimination. (Granted, it was a bit peripheral, but that's not so uncommon for first-years and their hypotheticals.) "How could you even bring that up?" the professor demanded. "It just belittles everything you've seen here!" Her tirade went on for a good two minutes, while my classmate sunk down into his chair, lowered his eyes, and said nothing.

The professor's response foreshadowed what too often passes for "open dialogue" at Boalt. Those on the far Left are entitled to say whatever they want, without regard for simple civility or for restraint in levying accusations. Those who disagree with them are to remain silent.

Of course this is a simplification of the situation at Boalt. In fact, I believe that many Boalt students who lean towards liberalism nevertheless would like to see a more balanced dialogue. But, frustratingly, not many will stand up for it. Nor will those on the Right. Why is it that we, as advocates in training, are nevertheless so reluctant to stand up for our positions?

Like most monopolists, the liberal voice at Boalt has achieved its position through unfair competition. One of the most powerful and destructive tools in silencing dissenting voices at Boalt is the casual use of various "isms." I am continually amazed by how easily certain students at Boalt will use one of their classmate's particular comments or political beliefs, without more, in order to label them racist or sexist. If you believe that disparate impact in and of itself isn't enough to constitute an Equal Protection violation (i.e., you agree with the Supreme Court's jurisprudence), then that is racism. If you, despite your well-intentioned, fine-toothed combing of the Constitution, just can't find a legal rule that says that veterans' preferences are impermissible gender discrimination, then that is sexism. If you think that these veterans' preferences are acceptable as a matter of policy – for the liberals who are willing to concede that there is a difference between constitutional permissibility and policy advisability – then that is *extreme* sexism. And woe to you if you believe that mothers on crack should lose their babies, you poor racist, sexist loser.

Holding any of these beliefs does not, in and of itself, make one a racist or a sexist. But expressing such beliefs in the classroom setting, with an acute awareness that certain of your classmates will use them to infer such traits about you, is really tough to do. When I say "infer," I don't mean to believe in a silent way. I have heard all of the above beliefs expressly called racist or sexist in the classroom. And if your classmate is publicly calling the beliefs that you hold racist or sexist, then it doesn't take a great inferential leap to recognize that your classmate is publicly calling you a racist or a sexist. No one wants to be called – or thought – such ugly things by their peers. As a result, many who disagree with the ultra-liberal viewpoint that dominates discussion at Boalt have learned to keep silent. I have tremendous respect for those who are brave enough to risk this unfair labeling in order to offer an alternative viewpoint, and I have tried my best to be among them. Still, there are times when it's just not worth it to speak out, and this is the much more common response at Boalt.

The silencing of the conservative voice at Boalt is no trivial matter. All voices deserve the chance to be heard and considered. It's a matter of respect and dignity for the individual. This is an argument long advanced by liberals, yet conveniently forgotten as applied to those who disagree with them.

The silencing of dissenting voices at Boalt also means that our classroom discussions are much less rich than they might otherwise be. In reading this article, maybe you have assumed that I am a conservative. I am not. I am a moderate Democrat. That my viewpoints can pass for conservatism in the classroom (which they sometimes do) appalls me and shows just how flat the debate is. Our expectations are anchored far to the Left at Boalt, and in most classes, we don't hear from true conservatives at all, only less extreme liberals. This lack of exchange is not only boring, it is antithetical to the educational mission of a university. The concept of a marketplace of ideas is based on the benefits of competition, from which the most meritorious ideas will emerge. But the liberal monopoly at Boalt has squelched the competition, and as monopolists tend to do, has left us with a product that is both costly and less than optimal.

During the Proposition 209 protest that took place on the first day of school this year, I listened to Professor Rachel Moran speak about how Boalt's entering class is less qualified than those of the past. She wondered how Boalt students could have an informed discussion about interpretive concepts such as probable cause and reasonable doubt without the input of African-American and other minorities who bring a unique perspective to the debate. She was absolutely right. Yet we continue to ignore, even silence, the conservative voice which is present at Boalt and which could also contribute to the richness of the debate. How can we expect to have an informed discussion about Proposition 209 when I have not heard – not once – anyone at Boalt publicly admit to supporting it? How shall we talk about gender discrimination in a class with only a few males? Once we leave Boalt, how shall we be effective lawyers, politicians, and businesspeople, when we have spent three years complete-ly isolated from the political tide that predominates our state?

The unfortunate result of this one-sidedness is that many Boalt students are completely ignorant of the arguments put forth on the Right, except in their grossest generalities. Whether your agenda is liberal or conservative, it pays to understand the other side. If the exchange were robust, we might even learn something.

Sadly, the liberal monopoly has made robust exchange a scarce good at Boalt. This is disappointing, because most of us in law school are relatively young, still trying out new ideas and testing the bounds of our beliefs. Yet this type of development requires a tolerant, for-giving atmosphere, one that allows for the full exploration of ideas, including directness, exaggeration, and even mistakes. But because no such atmosphere exists at Boalt, students are rarely willing to put their necks on the line. Knowing that what you say can and will be used against you makes students very careful – too careful – about what they say. They cautiously state just enough to get a point across, lest any passionate overstepping forever be ascribed to their belief sys-tem, rather than viewed as what it was meant to be – an exploration. So discussion is couched, watered-down at Boalt. We have "debate-lite." In our quest to all just get along, we avoid the controversial, especially challenges to the liberal hegemony. Our behavior is more like that of polite dinner guests than that of law students. This self-imposed reservedness is every bit as inhibiting to our development as is the lack of dialogue along the political spectrum.

In all fairness, some professors do try to encourage a more vig-orous, balanced discussion. For example, I am currently in a gender discrimination class with Professor Linda Krieger. While she comes at the issues from a liberal perspective, she has made clear from the beginning that alternative points of view are welcome. But so far, we haven't had many takers. This has to do with the composition of the class itself. We have only three men in the course, and I don't think it's going out on a limb to say that none of them are conservatives. Any true conservative has long since been scared away from even walking in to any course at Boalt on discrimination, because the type of tolerance Professor Krieger proposes is almost nonexistent at

Boalt. As a consequence, her offer of tolerance for diverse viewpoints falls flat on homogeneous ears.

Of course, it's easy to say that men just aren't interested in a class on gender discrimination, whites just aren't interested in a course on critical race theory. But this doesn't ring true with my experience. Many men and many whites at Boalt would like to take discrimination classes; it is an interesting and evolving area of the law. Yet, the conservatives among these groups are fearful of exposing themselves to an atmosphere in which their ideas, and sometimes even their presence, is not welcome. So, while the vast majority of corporations and law firms are headed by conservative males, we have none in our class on gender discrimination. Those who could learn the most from the class never walk in the door. Professors teaching discrimination law go on preaching to the choir, and the ideological gap at Boalt continues to widen.

This brings me to my final point about why the lack of dialogue between liberals and conservatives at Boalt is critical. It has created division where there might otherwise be tremendous opportunities for alliances. For example, many people at Boalt believe adamantly in the importance of having strong minority representation in the law school. You would think that this would lead to coalition-building around the Proposition 209 issue. Instead, the most extreme at Boalt organized the movement and engaged in activities that alienated most of their initial supporters, and I count myself among that group. While I endorse efforts to increase minority enrollment at Boalt, there was no way I was going to stand in the Dean's office and shout down a woman who has devoted a lifetime to defending the rights of women and minorities. Nor would I barge into first-year classrooms asking white men to give up their seats. Such actions make misguided, unfair accusations. But there was no room for dialogue between the extreme voices and those of moderation.

This typifies the "either you're with us or you're against us" attitude that characterizes the far Left at Boalt. These monopolists have bundled their practices, and either you buy them all, or you are not welcome to participate. In this way, the same unwillingness to engage in dialogue, restraint, and compromise that has hindered classroom exchange at Boalt has infected Boalt's political movements as well. Of course, all the blame cannot lie with the Left. During the objectionable protest activities, the moderates engaged in their usual silence, lacking the guts to stand up and say, "No, that is wrong." Instead, they quietly distanced themselves from the movement. A great opportunity for political alliance was lost.

Currently, the divide between liberals and conservatives at Boalt causes suspicion on the Left, and resentment on the Right. Yet imagine a Boalt where these differences instead produced a rich exchange, fostering respect for individual viewpoints, learning and enlightenment in the classroom, and productive political alliances. I have no easy answers about how to get there, and I am quite certain that no easy answers exist. Yet, there are steps we can take to change.

More conservatives must be willing to express their viewpoints in class, in spite of their fears of being demonized. Should the debate become one-sided nevertheless, more liberals and moderates need to offer alternative perspectives, even if that means playing devil's advocate.

In addition, we must all use restraint in our use of the various "isms," and in our tendency to hurl accusations. I sometimes think that activists at Boalt think they have succeeded when they have silenced the other side. I have indeed learned much from liberal classmates at Boalt – about unconscious racism, about supposedly neutral legal and social standards, and about different perspectives in general. But when I think about the moments that produced this learning, they were either moments of dialogue or of quiet self-reflection. Never were they moments of racially charged debate, for it seems to me that very little deep learning occurs from a defensive posture. When you call your classmate's views racist or sexist, he naturally becomes defensive. Take on his viewpoints with counter-arguments, not with convenient labels. And despite the fact that law school has instilled in us the litigator's value of debate, remember that discussion, not debate, is often a more effective tool for enlightening a colleague.

I do not mean to suggest that enlightenment, or agreement, should be the ultimate goal. One of the traditional, annoying, and arrogant aspects of conservatism is the idea that liberals are naive idealists, who will see the wisdom of conservatism once they learn the ways of the world. The far Left at Boalt suffers from a similar annoying arrogance. They seem to think that conservatives are ignorant of the perspectives of the oppressed and would come around to a better view if only they were more enlightened people. Perhaps that is why some Boalt liberals have deemed a "be silent and listen" agenda appropriate. But just as liberalism is not necessarily a product of naiveté, neither is conservatism necessarily a product of ignorance. Well-informed people disagree. That is the richness of the marketplace of ideas, a richness we should celebrate, not suppress.

Professors, you, too, have an important role. Make clear at the outset of your courses that diverse viewpoints are valued, repeat the offer throughout the course, and be sure you live up to it by encouraging those who do offer competing perspectives. If you sense a dearth of discussion on one side of an issue, then play devil's advocate and prompt it. If you see a student engaging in the type of accusations that will stifle debate, then discourage this behavior. Many of you have learned to be effective moderators of discussion, but more of you could learn to be better facilitators. You have colleagues – for example, Professor Jesse Choper – who are masters of this art, so learn from their expertise.

I certainly do not mean to imply that every course or discussion must be ideologically balanced. It would be ludicrous, for example, to expect that a course in critical race theory would be so, since a political perspective is inherent in the material. You as professors have your own perspectives, and by all means you should teach from them. But the richness of your scholarship can only be improved by contrasting it with competing assumptions, exposing its flaws, and highlighting its strengths. You professors who teach courses that traditionally scare away conservatives (or liberals) have a special duty to be proactive to recruit and welcome them. If nothing else, I guarantee it will enliven your teaching experience.

We cannot rely on the bravery of conservatives or the self-restraint of liberals to solve the problem in its entirety. Nor can professors play the facilitator role alone. Each and every one of us has a responsibility to maintain the conditions that foster open dialogue – conditions of civility and tolerance for diverse viewpoints, including conservative ones. Maintaining these conditions includes admonishing those who violate them. It isn't easy to censure your classmates when they make statements or accusations that silence dialogue. Yet, we as Boalt students manage to enforce all kinds of informal norms in the classroom. Witness the demise of most of the red-hots (those who talk to hear themselves speak) after the first year. Let's add civility and tolerance to the list of norms we demand of one another.

One of the biggest obstacles so far in accomplishing this goal has been guilt – white guilt, male guilt, whatever you want to call it. Because the voices of women and minorities have been silenced for so long, and because these groups are feeling attacked by California's current political climate, we are reluctant to censure members of these groups, even when they do cross the lines of civility. Perhaps we even worry that those lines of civility are the ones drawn by the dominant culture, and that they might not be the same for other groups. I believe that this reluctance and fear are why some of the activities of the Proposition 209 protest, which offended many people's sense of fairness, nevertheless failed to draw much public criticism at Boalt (though they drew a lot of criticism in hushed voices).

In short, at Boalt we tolerate more extreme behavior from women and minorities and those advocating on their behalf than we do from other individuals. Maybe this is right in some degree – I'm not sure – but it is not right when applied without bounds. Discouraging the incivilities and accusations that stifle classroom debate while maintaining a healthy respect for our historical inattention to the voices of women and minorities is a difficult balancing act. But we must not give up on the task, allowing the voices of an extreme few to silence dialogue among many.

I hope that all groups at Boalt, including the far Left, will view the current situation as an opportunity for positive change. For unlike a monopolist in the marketplace of goods, the monopolist in the marketplace of ideas suffers alongside those whose voices have been silenced. A free and open marketplace of ideas benefits all without regard to ideology.

The Usuals

By Anne Hawkins

It started out, for me, as almost a joke. I would keep track in class of the comments those "conservative" individuals made, and then I would quickly jot down the response coming from those "liberal" individuals. It got to the point where I could close my eyes and know not only what comments were coming next, but exactly whose hands shot up in response to each consecutive assertion. Initially, I was intrigued. Coming straight out of a politically correct undergraduate education, I was amazed that people actually openly voiced "Republican" viewpoints. In addition, I was happy to realize that in the midst of all the commotion of Boalt's newfound homogeneity that there really were a variety of viewpoints being expressed.

But the joke of knowing exactly who disagreed with whom soon turned into serious discontent. By late October of my first year, I realized that I needed to sit down and consider the reasons why I was so incredibly dissatisfied with my law school experience. After talking to a few deans at other law schools in an attempt to decide whether transferring was the answer to my problems, I realized that it wasn't the course material at school that bothered me. It was the manner in which class discussions dealt with it.

I realize as I sit in class that I have yet to speak voluntarily in any class this year. But, that isn't a comment on my level of comfort in class. Rather, it is an indication of how I feel my classmates would respond, or more likely not respond to what I might have to offer. I listen everyday in class to people vehemently articulate their points of view. In fact, I listen to the same people every day holding conversations with themselves, and never stopping to consider that someone else in the class who might stand on the opposite side of the political spectrum, or may not even exist on the spectrum at all, could actually have something valid to say. I listen as people argue with each other, but essentially make the same point. I get frustrated because I hear the same things every day, back and forth. Yet, I wonder if we would all just stop and actually listen to the words we are saying, instead of assuming that everyone else is automatically wrong, if we would cease the repetition and actually make some progress.

I continually hear people at Boalt say that there is a need for open dialogue and an open exchange of ideas. For me, this "progressive" idea was easy to digest, until I realized that acceptance of all viewpoints isn't exactly what these people have in mind. It's okay to talk about how certain minority groups have been oppressed. It's okay to point out that illiterates and the poor sometimes need special protection. But, it's not okay to point out that not all landlords are richer than their tenants or that sometimes when small businesses come out on the losing end of a contract it isn't necessarily due to bad faith on the part of the big business.

There are many times in class when I disagree with a comment someone makes. Unlike some of my conservative classmates, when the Supreme Court protects a woman's right to choose, I don't see it as condoning murder. I don't agree that housewives who are divorced by their husbands and left without any marketable skills and economic means to support their children simply assumed the risk when they got married and chose to stay home. At the same time, I don't think that every poor person, every minority, every woman or every homosexual in the cases we read has always been wronged by a paternalistic oppressive system.

So, I still sit in class and laugh at how ridiculous the dialogue is. For the most part, it is open and there are a variety of viewpoints being expressed. More often than not I learn something new, or see a different way of approaching a situation. But every day I leave class wondering if those people who continually raise their hands are so focused on hearing their own voices that they fail to listen to the voices of others. I wonder if they are so concerned with contradicting certain individuals that they will never stop to acknowledge that underneath all the presentation, every single person has a legitimate point of view worth listening to. Though many people are quick to say that they want an atmosphere conducive to the open exchange of ideas, I question how seriously those same people have thought about the fact that if they want others to consider and potentially accept their statements as valid, at some point they, too, will have to stop and consider what other people have to say.

A Call for Respect
By Jim Culp

I was at first hesitant when David Wienir suggested I share my experiences with diversity at Boalt Hall. A white man, I firmly advocate affirmative action, and I initially thought I could add little insight to David's project. But I talked with David, and we listened to one another, and I discovered that we had shared a very similar experience during our time at Boalt. I am grateful to him for giving me the opportunity to share my experiences. I am similarly thankful to Mike Jaurigue, a former marine, a fellow law student, a Filipino, and a leader in the movement to maintain a diverse student body at Boalt Hall. He is the best friend and mentor I have ever known, and I have learned much that I know about diversity and equality from him.

As a young boy I once asked my father what it meant to be deaf and dumb. He told me that being deaf is when people "hear what they want to hear," and being "dumb," he said, "is why they do it." Well, I believe that diversity is a little deaf and dumb at Boalt Hall. I am a third-year law student at the law school, and this is a message that I will take with me when I graduate in the spring. I chose Boalt Hall over other law schools for its reputation as an institution devoted to a diverse student body and the free flow of ideas. I don't believe the latter can exist without the former. Yet, in my three years here at Boalt Hall, I have discovered the reverse is not true. As I have witnessed, Boalt Hall, though arguably diverse, is marked by a lack of tolerance and freedom of expression. Judge for yourself.

I had my first confrontation with the intolerant diversity and tyranny of political correctness at Boalt Hall in my first semester during a tort lecture. The discussion for the day was the tort of intentional infliction of emotional distress. The professor informed the class that courts do not allow this cause of action between man and wife. In the professor's opinion, the reason for the courts' view was that emotional distress is an inherent component of married life and, upon entering the union, both man and wife somehow "assumed the risk" of emotional distress (the professor is single). I audibly snickered at the remark and quickly learned that I was the only person who had seen the humor in it (I am married). Ugly stares were cast in my direction from many of the hundred or so students in the class.

At this point I knew that the discussion was just getting interesting, and the glares of indiscretion from my classmates awoke my lust for inflaming the intolerant. My chance to be honest and controversial came quickly thereafter. The professor invited commentary from the class in regards to disallowing intentional infliction of emotional distress claims in the domestic arena.

A female Yale graduate quickly offered her opinion. "I see this as a major step backwards for women," she asserted. "We have come too far for the courts to ignore the fact that mental abuse of women is as harmful and brutal as physical abuse." Her gender-specific take on the issue was more than I could bear. Like many others, I raised my hand to respond.

As the professor looked over his options and saw my hand, he unsuccessfully tried to conceal his smile. "How do you feel about this Mr. Culp?" he asked. As my peers turned in my direction, I noticed the ugly glances had returned. "Well," I said, "I have five sisters, a mother, two grandmothers and a wife, and I don't feel that men have a monopoly on inflicting emotional distress. In fact, I have come to believe that women are better at it than men. Hence, unlike physical abuse, inflicting emotional distress is not an issue specific to women, as men and women are equally perpetrators and victims of it."

There was a roar of scorn from many women in the class. Many stood up screaming unintelligible insults. Some even threw objects at me. In one swoop I had successfully defined myself as a misogynist and chauvinist. For months groups of women would snicker as I walked by. Though some of the students in the class, both men and women of all races and ethnicities, dared to listen to what I meant that day (and later became some of my closest friends in law school), most did not. I had unknowingly become the male-pig poster child for the militant feminists at Boalt Hall.

But feminists at Boalt Hall are not unique in their unwillingness to listen to others. Many minority students have likewise demonstrated that racism is not open for discussion at the law school. The clearest example of this occurred during a criminal law lecture. I have to begin retelling this experience by first describing my criminal law professor, who will be etched forever in my mind. Though a rather small and elderly man, he appeared to me from our first class to be somewhat larger than life. His wisdom (he has won many national awards, was a former dean of Boalt Hall, and authored the textbook used in our class) and his respectful, caring and gentle manner reminded me each class why I wanted to become a lawyer. I remember that, before he began each lecture, he would look intently about the classroom at us, his students. In his eyes I could always see that we were the reason he was a professor. These characteristics, as well as the fact that he is Jewish, are important factors in understanding the following recount of one of the saddest days of my law school experience.

The lecture that day concerned the Bernhard Goetz case and what factors may be considered in determining whether a person has the requisite "reasonable fear" to justify using lethal force in self-defense. The lecture basically concerned the following question: "If all murders are committed by 'purple' people, may a person's 'reasonable fear' be based partly on the fact that she finds herself in the midst of 'purple' people?" Of course the question, like most law school questions, has no right answer. On the one hand, it seems unreasonable to preclude a person from considering race in such a situation. On the other hand, even if all murders are committed by purple people, not all purple people commit murders.

The professor discussed the conundrum, and then attempted to share with the class a personal experience relating to the problem. Without going into the details of the story, the professor basically found himself in the purple people situation discussed above and modified his behavior based partly on a potential aggressor's race. The professor then went on to say that although the experience had taken place many years previous, he is still bothered by his reaction to the situation. Now, remember that this man is both Jewish and old enough to have been a young man during the Holocaust.

Well, to put it mildly, what happened next disgusts me to this day. The professor asked for opinions concerning his experience and he was verbally attacked by several minority students. In ugly tones they called him, amongst other things, a "racist," and characterized his behavior as everything that is evil. I believe tears welled up in his eyes, and then he simply replied that he didn't think he would share such experiences with students in the future. I can say no more about that day, other than that it was simply the worst example of disrespect and ignorance I had ever witnessed. I will never forgive myself for not saying as much on the spot.

Disrespect seems to be the overall theme for diversity at Boalt Hall: people disrespecting people. It is why students, and people in general don't listen, it's why they don't care, and it's a major underlying cause for discrimination and oppression. I always tell people that if their purpose is to effect change, then reach out to their audience with respect and they will be heard, not by all, but they will be heard. On the other hand, if their goal is to feel some therapeutic release of anger, then get up as high as they can on their soap box and attack everyone within earshot. But don't be surprised when the audience becomes defensive and attacks back. There are too many soap box speakers on diversity issues at Boalt Hall, and I am left to wonder how many future allies of the diversity cause were lost during their time at the law school. Shame on all those who take a place at Boalt Hall but aren't smart enough to put the good of their cause before their personal agenda.

The topic of shame brings me to the final example of Boalt Hall's special kind of disrespectful diversity. I am an Army veteran who, as a paratrooper, jumped out of airplanes in the middle of the night in foreign lands before most of my peers at Boalt Hall had reached puberty. I must admit that I have little tolerance for the disrespect, ignorance, and hypocrisy that many students at Boalt Hall demonstrate toward the military because of the "don't ask, don't tell" policy. Each year Military JAG representatives come to Boalt Hall to recruit young lawyers into the service. These men and women members of the military come to the law school and are subjected to demonstrations denouncing the military and the men and women who serve in it.

I believe there are a couple of universal truths that apply to those who have participated in these demonstrations. First, none of them know the meaning of sacrifice, and they disgrace all those who have done so in the past, including many homosexual servicemen and servicewomen who put their need to openly share their sexual orientation behind their desire to serve this nation. I have occasionally been asked whether I believe I ever shared a foxhole with a homosexual. I always answer, "I don't care, any of them would have given their life for me." On the other hand, I honestly would never desire to share a foxhole with any of the students at Boalt Hall who have participated in these anti-military demonstrations, regardless of their sexual preference.

Secondly, like most of the "soap box" proponents of diversity at Boalt Hall who graduate, take $100,000 jobs in law firms, and become members of the establishment, too frequently the protesters don't mean what they say. Too frequently they don't "really" care about the issue. How many have written letters to or have gone to speak with those who make the laws in this country? Far too few. Rather, the protesters choose to attack those who serve instead of communicating with those who make policy.

I will soon graduate from law school, and these are the experiences I will remember when I reflect back on diversity at Boalt Hall. I can only hope that other future leaders approach the issue of diversity differently and more effectively than many at Boalt Hall have done. I will be a father in a few months, and I want my child to have the opportunity, as I did, to attend schools that are full of different types of people and ideas. Like others who will effect positive change in this country, I hope my child will be respectful, listen, and learn.

CHAPTER THREE

THE MUDDLED GOALS OF DIVERSITY

When the idea of diversity is not freely investigated, and when dialogue is stifled, in the ways described in the last two chapters, the meaning of diversity becomes confused, and the goals of diversity become muddled. And when one group in a community uses its considerable power to define diversity exclusively in its expedient terms, minorities themselves begin to suffer, as the contributors in this chapter describe.

We All Belong Here

By Isabelle Quinn

The segregation that occurred in my childhood was created by housing restrictions. As was typical at that time, my parents were required to sign papers when they bought their home, promising never to sell to "Negroes," "Filipinos," or other "Orientals." The fact that my parents themselves were Filipino immigrants never became a real issue while I was growing up because they were also of European descent. This gave my family the advantage of "passing" such segregation roadblocks.

After the desegregation of the sixties, my high school became integrated. Although desegregation technically removed ethnic and racial barriers to housing, I still got on the school bus in a white neighborhood. As that neighborhood eventually began to change, I became acutely aware of the phenomenon of "integration" as it actually played out and of "diversity" – although then, we did not use the latter term.

As a student, I embraced the political ideals of the sixties and I felt that most students were similarly very liberal in their attitudes toward the civil rights of minority groups, at least in theory. Yet, in hindsight, I see that the practical effect of integration was that we still closely associated with the same people as before and that we still segregated ourselves, consciously or unconsciously, in terms of familiar patterns. Even though I felt like a cultural bridge to newly immigrated Filipinos, I looked like one of "the others" to them and was not really accepted. At the time, my efforts at multicultural exchange were seen as "cool" by my white friends, but it did not have much practical effect, since both groups still chose to sit apart.

When I graduated high school and attended Berkeley as an undergraduate, the minority groups there were not segregated from an outsider's viewpoint as they had been in high school. I easily made many new friends who were from diverse ethnic and racial backgrounds. In hindsight, however, I ask myself whether such numerical integration can ever really promote diversity.

At Berkeley, I suddenly seemed to be exposed to a whole new section of minority students who appeared to have very much in common with most of the white students I knew, both in educational background and in world viewpoints. Also, it seemed that an awareness of what was "politically correct" was universal. Further, when thinking back to my classroom experiences at Berkeley, I do not remember much, if any, multicultural influence or exchange, either in terms of curricular choices or of general classroom discussions. When ethnic minorities spoke up in class, for instance, I do not remember there being anything culturally innovative or enlightening about their views or discussion.

Today, I ask whether the traditional framework of the Berkeley curriculum at that time allowed for much divergence in ideas and whether the student selection process created numerical diversity, while actually promoting uniformity in views. On the other hand, people with different views may simply have been discouraged from speaking up.

Now, after more than twenty years since studying as an undergraduate at Berkeley, I ask myself the very same questions and wonder if today's Berkeley classroom has really changed. Is the goal of "diversity" different? Is it a method, a result, both? As was the case then, most students I talk to still define diversity in terms of numbers; the success of the goal of diversity is expressed in terms of how many minorities are here and how many graduate.

However, on appearance, I am viewed as a white student, not as a member of a minority group, and I am viewed as an older conservative student, not as a moderate or liberal. This view caused a class-mate to call me a "racist white conservative idiot," when I expressed my outrage at being asked to give up my seat to a minority at a recent classroom protest staged in support of affirmative action. The irony of this was that when I first entered Berkeley, I benefited from affirmative action, protested in support of minority students at the time, and, today, still support the idea of diversity.

Although the continued emphasis on concrete numerical results in affirmative action does not appear to have changed since the 70's, students at Boalt Hall today do seem very aware that integration alone has not been effective and, as a result, are looking for additional solutions to achieve diversity. In this regard, they are overlooking something they can each do right now. All students can become more proficient in their ability to recognize and to understand the diversity that already exists among us, while at the same time working toward changes.

At Boalt Hall today there remains a problem created by the goal of preserving a high academic standard and reputation within a fundamentally traditional educational framework. An ethnically "diverse" student enrollment, no matter how it is eventually achieved, may not even begin to reflect the diversity that actually exists within groups, if these people are not encouraged to speak up. In turn, there is also a lack of ability to encourage the expression of diversity between groups. In this respect, I believe the views expressed in my law classes today are still predominately the popular "socially acceptable" views within the available curricular framework – just like twenty years ago. For me, that is an expression of uniformity, rather than diversity.

So what do I feel has changed most in twenty years? People like me are just more aware of what is or is not politically correct to say in class. If I strongly disagree with a popular view, I know that most efforts to express myself will be unrewarding. Also, my experience has been that people are often so concerned with what they want to say next, that they do not effectively listen. What is needed to address this is to acquire an ability to preface one's own view with an acknowledgment and understanding of the other person's viewpoint.

For instance, to simply say "I can see that would be effective if..." or "Yes, I can understand your concern that...," before one expresses one's disagreement, would be a method to positively reinforce the expression of diversity within the classroom.

We do not always have the luxury of dealing with people who agree with us. What the speaker of an unpopular view at Berkeley learns to do very quickly when faced with only negative response is to shut up in the future. As an older re-entry student, the result of feeling isolated by my views is not particularly disturbing to me; most of my social acquaintances are outside of school anyway. However, if one purports to truly support diversity, then alternative views – even if very different from one's own – should be positively encouraged. Only then will we be able to really welcome all people and to benefit from the heterogeneity of all groups, including minorities. In this, students at Berkeley today have no more skill than did their counterparts of the sixties.

In class at Boalt Hall, one can sometimes feel like an invited guest at dinner. One's table manners must be adjusted to fit politely within an acceptable range of social etiquette or one is viewed as an uneducated boor. Furthermore, one's personal preferences must conform to eating the available meal without criticism, with the place settings at hand, and in the fashion displayed by the host or one is reminded that they are not at home. For myself, I would rather see people encouraged to eat with their fingers, if they prefer, or to throw the occasional bone. In this, all students and instructors can play a more active role. No student enrolled at Boalt is an invited guest. We all belong here.

Vanishing Diversity
By Daryl Singhi

The first year at Boalt Hall presented some interesting lessons that I did not expect to learn in law school. Early on I began to feel that a school with such a legacy of open-mindedness does not necessarily afford that luxury to all of its students. I had thought that I would meet people of varying backgrounds, experiences, and opinions. I hoped that some of these things would stimulate, provoke, or even enrage me. There are many that would say that such things couldn't be present without a diverse student body. This makes sense, but when the diversity is to be delineated strictly by ethnic and racial characteristics, I have some doubts. I chose Boalt in order to hear and be heard, but that just didn't happen.

On the first day of orientation the students of the Class of 2000 met each other. The speeches by the administration emphasized teamwork and cooperation to get the most out of the law school experience. When we broke into our small sections that we would be working with all year, the friendliness continued. Introductions were cordial and every single person was getting along. Once classes began, and political or social biases began to surface, things began to change.

Quickly, whom you associated with became more indicative of your opinions than what you actually said. That a man is white, or a woman is black, does not predestine their political or social beliefs. Statistics can point to tendencies, but in such a small sample size as found in the Class of 2000, the numbers are meaningless. I appear to be a white male, and among the people I befriended at Boalt were some conservative students. That I am actually an Asian-American and was brought up in a multicultural household did nothing to overshadow the connection between those conservative thinkers and me. Diversity was staring directly at those who desired it, but instead of cherishing and respecting it, all it was accorded was spite.

It is fine to castigate somebody for having an opinion that stands in the face of yours, but it is another matter to lob personal attacks to debase the person instead of their thoughts. Rumors and innuendo pervaded the campus. "Terrorist," "sexist," "white supremacist," and "racist" were all terms used as commentary on various individuals. Now it was all "sides" involved in this mess, and for that I am truly embarrassed for the Class of 2000.

As time went on, peaceful coexistence became the norm, and most involved in the early turmoil at Boalt Hall began to just tune out the words of those that opposed them – and those that they thought opposed them. I am sure that many of the entering class had come to Boalt Hall, like I had, to enjoy an environment where ideas and experiences were exchanged freely. These things vanished before our eyes.

Minority Views Are in the Majority
By Jennifer Wood

"**O**ur education is being compromised! Minority views are absent in classroom discussions!" These accusations are part of the dialogue engaged in by the opponents of Proposition 209. When students at Boalt realized that only one African-American was part of the Class of 2000, they accused the administration of not protecting the quality of education at Boalt. They asserted that a lack of minority students at Boalt would compromise education. They further asserted that the Class of 2000 would be unprepared when it graduated because "minority views" will be absent from classroom discussion. I find this argument to be disturbing in many ways. The term "minority viewpoint" is problematic. This essay attempts to clarify a number of potential meanings of the term "minority viewpoint."

First, the term "minority viewpoint" could be used to mean any idea expressed by a minority student. This definition is unsatisfying because it does not suggest anything that makes these ideas essential to a legal education. The study of law is about learning how the law currently works and discussing how it should work. Almost every law student has an opinion on legal issues, but they are not all critical to a complete legal education.

Typically, in any legal issue, there is a core group of theories and multiple variations on those themes. Possibly because minorities are underrepresented in the legal profession, the opinions of this group are especially important to a legal education. However, this suggests that they think as a group and cannot have individual opinions of their own. If the threat which is so feared by affirmative action activists is that their legal education is being compromised by a lack of minority viewpoints, there has to be something inherently different about a "minority viewpoint" that is not present in a non-minority viewpoint. However, this would lead us to a different, second, definition of a minority viewpoint.

That is, the term "minority viewpoint" could be used to mean that minorities, due to their experience in society, necessarily have a different perspective on the law than non-minority students. However, this is also problematic – people of the same race can disagree about substantive legal issues, including issues concerning race. Does Clarence Thomas hold a "minority viewpoint" regarding affirmative action? He doesn't believe in affirmative action, and many African-Americans disagree with the position he holds on this issue, yet they are all African-American.

Activists crying out about a lack of minority viewpoints have yet to explain why two African-Americans disagreeing over affirmative action is any different from two students of any other race disagreeing. A professor is quoted asking: "How can you teach *Brown v. Board of Education* without any African-American students in the room?" Taken at face value that comment suggests that a room full of white, Asian, and Hispanic students would not be able to flush out the competing interests and arguments in a historical context without an African-American in the room. That is really offensive. It further puts an expectation on the African-American student to speak up as a representative of an entire race and give the "minority viewpoint." For it assumes that everyone else's education would be compromised without it.

Within the first month of school in the fall of 1997, a letter was passed around on behalf of the Class of 2000 in support of affirmative action. The letter affirmatively asserted that the students' education was being "compromised" by the race-blind admission policy. More than two-thirds of first-years signed it. Where are the majority of California voters who passed Proposition 209? Where are the Republicans? If there are views missing from discussion, it is those of conservative students.

Berkeley, because of its revolutionary reputation, attracts liberal students. This leaves it at a disadvantage in recruiting conservative law students. Rarely, if ever, in classroom discussion has any student spoken up on behalf of the religious Right. Often the religious Right is condemned. As a significant portion of the population in the country, their views should be voiced in discussion, yet nobody seems concerned about the absence of these views from discussion.

The reality of the situation is that although there may not be as many minority students in the first-year class as in previous years, classroom discussion is as fruitful as ever. Non-minority students often bring into discussion how the law or policy affects underrepresented people in society. If any views are missing from classroom discussion at Boalt, they are not "minority viewpoints."

Regardless of whether "minority viewpoints" indicates any comment made by a minority student, or a view molded by a unique experience in society, they will never be absent from classroom discussion at Boalt. So long as Boalt continues to have excellent professors and attract top students, the discussion in classrooms will always be diverse. The demise of affirmative action has many consequences for Boalt, but a decrease in the quality of education is not one of them.

CHAPTER FOUR

CUFFED BY THE THOUGHT-POLICE

Could there be any worse detriment to
a legal education than students feeling
that their opinions, no matter how civil,
are not at all welcome? Most of the
voices in this chapter would answer a
resounding "yes." It is one thing to be
unwelcome, another to be attacked
personally for intellectual views that
have been purposefully distorted. Even
worse, however, as these writers describe,
is the concerted effort by a small number
of people in an academic community to
threaten the right of free speech of
countless others.

Of Vandals and Cowards
By Catharine Bailey

Recently, a series of events has occurred unbeknownst to most members of the Boalt Hall community. These events disgrace our school and prove the presence of the very problem this publication seeks to address – the problem of intellectual cowardice at Boalt. As a Federalist Society officer, it is my responsibility to publicize all events sponsored by the Society. This includes stuffing mailboxes, distributing flyers, and maintaining our bulletin board. (Yes, we have a bulletin board, located in the far depths of the law school at the opposite end of the hallway in which the Office of Career Services is located. You may notice the space given to us by the school is as far away from visibility as possible, unlike the bulletin board of Boalt Democrats.)

During the week of February 22, 1998, I spent a few hours designing a series of flyers for our upcoming semester events and placing fifty or so flyers on all Boalt public bulletin boards and on our own bulletin board. This was benign material advertising a debate on education reform, talks on forfeiture laws and Miranda rights, and a late semester cocktail party for members – not exactly incendiary speech. When I placed these flyers on the public boards, I made a point not to cover the flyers of other groups, but attempted to share space equitably. After all, I value freedom of expression and want my fellow students to be able to make informed choices about events at Boalt.

The next day, the first act of cowardice occurred. Much to my surprise, every single flyer was torn down from every board. Even the flyers on The Federalist Society Board and other remote public boards were gone, although other flyers on the same boards were left untouched. This cowardice was not a onetime event. I promptly redistributed the flyers to each public board and our own. Later that same day, the flyers were torn off again. And again I tried, this time stapling the flyers with as many staples as possible and adding more tacks. Sure enough, everything was torn down.

The most egregious act of cowardice came shortly thereafter. I placed flyers on our board and public boards publicizing the Choper-Pilon debate on judicial activism, with "sponsored by the Boalt Hall Federalist Society" in small print at the bottom. When I placed these on our basement bulletin board, I included a note saying: "Please do not tear these flyers down. Doing so is an awful waste of time, money, and paper, not to mention a little petty. Instead, we invite you to attend one of our meetings and try to debunk us, or simply ignore us. Thank You." The next day, not only were the flyers ripped from their staples, but the entire backdrop of the bulletin board, including The Federalist Society sign, was ripped off.* Not only a demonstration of cowardice, but also vandalism.

At first, I was just surprised. I know The Federalist Society does not draw huge crowds at every meeting and that the political views its members tend to espouse are not widely endorsed by Boalt students. But, I did not think that someone at Boalt – or any law school, for that matter – would be so childish and petty. After all, we are adults who may be called upon to defend First Amendment speech rights or to advocate issues on the merits, rather than run away from or try to hide contrary or even unpleasant points of view.

---

* Editors' Note: A memorandum was sent on April 3, 1998 from Dean Herma Hill Kay to the Boalt community after The Federalist Society bulletin board was defaced and torn off the wall. The memorandum, which refers to the vandalism against The Federalist Society without naming it, addresses "acts of disrespect" at Boalt Hall that "threaten the academic environment, which can thrive only when ideas are freely exchanged and encouraged." See Appendix C.

Then I was mad. "What a coward," I thought. Some person in the Boalt community was such a coward that he or she had to waste time tearing down bland flyers which few people would see anyway, rather than attend our meetings and try to argue rationally and maturely against our views. Someone was so afraid that a student would see our flyers, have an interest in the topic, attend a meeting, and actually see there is more than the "liberal" viewpoint on important legal matters.

I also thought of how hypocritical this person must be. It is highly probable, given the number of students who do not support Proposition 209, this person is supportive of affirmative action. It is also highly probable that the person holds these views on the ground that not having higher numbers of people with a certain skin color attending Boalt jeopardizes our exposure to a diversity of experiences and viewpoints, and inhibits our ability to be effective, well-educated citizens and advocates. Yet, this person is doing precisely what he or she likely claims 209 does – stifling a minority and an opportunity for Boalt students to be better informed and prepared to represent clients against a variety of arguments. Chances are that this person is supportive of recycling. However, his or her actions have compelled me to duplicate three times the copies of flyers as necessary and to start stuffing each mailbox with individual notices – a wasteful practice we had hoped to avoid.

To the Coward: You won't be able to win arguments by stealing your opponent's brief, shoving cotton in the judge's ears, or stuffing a sock in a witness's mouth. You do a disservice to yourself and others by not exposing yourself to different viewpoints and advocating on the merits. One more thing: Thank you – you wasted your time, plenty of paper, and student activities fees from your own tuition money to fund our additional copies. You also strengthened our resolve, disgraced the school and those with whom you associate, and gave us a reason to use more intrusive publicity methods, such as sending broadcast e-mails and stuffing mail boxes. Thanks also for the publicity. You also have given us strong ammunition to get a more prominently placed bulletin board which no one can miss seeing.

You also proved our point, that there are plenty of opportunities for one to express a viewpoint at Boalt, but not any viewpoint you don't espouse.

To the Boalt Community: Don't let this person disgrace us all. If you see someone doing this, do not hesitate to remind them of their cowardice and immaturity. Remind them of the reasons so many students are upset about Proposition 209. Remind them that we cannot be proud of a school where someone can do this, where we can't say who we are, what we believe, and what events we are sponsoring. Remind them that we are striving to be honorable members of an honorable profession, not vandals and cowards.

News From the Ladies' Room
By Megan Elizabeth Murray

This piece was written from my heart. It is not prize-winning writing. It is not first-rate story-telling. It is how I feel, poured out onto paper with little editing. It is the true experience of a second-year Boalt Hall student.

Diversity. What a joke. Webster's dictionary defines diversity as, "quality, state, fact, or instance of being different or dissimilar; varied." Boalt diverse? Not even close. On the biggest issue facing the university today, affirmative action, only one voice is heard. That is the voice of the tyrannical few.

Boalt is the most homogenous place I have been. Everywhere I look I see signs and stickers about the racist regime of Proposition 209. In every class I hear how each and every regulatory scheme is racist – even organ transplant distribution schemes (how dare they prefer donees with the same blood type?). Half the student body wears T-shirts that say "Educate, Don't Segregate." I do not believe a word of it. Yet, I virtually never speak up. Why is that? I am one of the most outspoken people around. I have never shied away from making outrageous remarks. I am the one who will shout out that the emperor is wearing no clothes. But for some reason, I stay silent at Boalt. I stay silent because the atmosphere is so hostile. I stay silent because the arguments are irrational.

The latest sign posted talks about declining minority admissions to the school. It says, and I really do quote, "No more of this shit." This is what is hanging in my face when I go to check my mailbox at school. The only thing I ever see in the weekly bulletin from the Dean's office to the students is that it is against school rules for anyone to remove such signs. There is never a word about the profanity or the attacking nature of the signs. So I get to walk around my own school with messages cursing about the racism of school policies. Of course, these same signs make no mention of the decline in applications from minorities. It is awfully hard to get admitted if you do not apply. However, I know that if I put up a sign mentioning that, it would be torn down in a heartbeat, and no one would do a thing about it.

There are other signs. There are ones referring to 209 as "racist legislation" and implying that all of us who voted for it are racist. Slap an ugly label like that on us, combine it with an irrational refusal to listen to opposing arguments, and none of us are going to speak.

The stickers have to be the best, though. In every bathroom stall, on almost every locker, and in all kinds of odd places, like the middle of walls, there are stickers again calling Proposition 209 racist, and rallying to support affirmative action. Stickers are not removed nearly as easily as posters. Believe me. I have tried. I have never been one to criticize others for speaking. All year I have fought the urge to tear these signs and posters and stickers off the walls. My feeling has been that it is everyone's prerogative to speak how they please. After many months it finally got to me, though, and I tried to take a sticker off the stall door in a bathroom. Forget it. They will have to be sanded off, literally.

I gave up for a while after that. I decided it was my conscience telling me it was the wrong thing to do. It was not my place. So I dropped it. A few weeks later, though, I got really steamed. In a stall, someone had partially torn off a sticker. It left a white sheet of backing paper behind. Someone had written on that sheet, "Affirmative action is racism." The next person had scribbled over it. What right did that person have, I thought, to cross it out? My whole philosophy of leaving everything behind had been premised on the belief that we all have a right to speak, but here the very people whose rights I was trying to respect were not respecting the rights of others. So, I stooped as low as I ever have. I wrote on the leftover sticker. I could not believe I did it, because I am one of those goody two-shoes who would never vandalize or deface property. I suppose I justified it by thinking that I only wrote on the sticker, not the wall. I still felt guilty, though. I did. I do not anymore.

What I wrote was, "You can't ignore the truth by scratching it out. Affirmative action is racism." I checked back a few weeks later. Someone had written, and again, I apologize for the profanity, "You fucking idiot! Prop. 209 allows the racist regime to continue." I stopped feeling guilty right then and there. Why have I been so careful in respecting the rights of people whose arguments consist of name-calling and profanity? I suddenly felt obligated to respond. Maybe that is what they wanted. I do not know. All I know is that suddenly, writing on the leftover sticker on a bathroom wall was not vandalism. It was almost a right I had to respond to being torn down.

So, I wrote back. First, I circled "fucking idiot" and wrote, "Brilliant," next to it. Then I went to the end of the last woman's message and wrote, "NO. Giving one race preference over another is RACISM." I used up the sticker on that message. I have not heard back. Maybe she feels the same way I do about vandalizing the wall. Maybe she can only bring herself to write on the sticker, too. Maybe I should bring in a new sticker. I would feel terrible about sticking it on in the first place though. They don't come off.

My bathroom experience sums up my frustration with the lack of true diversity at Boalt. How can we call the school diverse when a segment of the population speaks out only in bathroom stalls? This school touts itself as one of the best in the country. How can that be when students are not truly free to speak and share ideas? How can meaningful intellectual discourse take place when every word is chosen so carefully so as not to offend? It cannot. How can a school claim to be one of the best when no meaningful discourse takes place? It cannot. Those of us who believe in Proposition 209, who believe that racial preference is racist, and who are proud card-carrying Republicans lurk about in the shadows. We are not holding rallies, wearing T-shirts, or posting profanity-filled signs. Yet we are here. You would not know it from listening in classes or reading posters around school, but we are here. True diversity can only come about if we come out of the stalls and show our faces.

We're All Losers
By Randall Lewis

As a whole, I do not feel intimidated to speak in class for fear of how the class might react. The atmosphere in the classroom at Boalt generally is conducive to honest discussion. Yet, the topic of race when entering the classroom is of such a nature that certain classes failed to hold rational discussions. During a criminal law class the discussion focused on whether clothing should be admissible evidence in court. Students in the class kept insisting that stereotyping is wrong per se; that one should never be judged on the clothes they wear. The professor tried to nudge the class to admit that theoretically clothing may make a difference. I had trouble accepting that clothing should never be admissible. I offered a hypothetical. Imagine a minority in the South upon seeing four men in white hooded robes. Wouldn't he be justified in stereotyping? I was not drawing an analogy between inner city youth wearing baggy jeans and KKK members wearing KKK garb. I was merely trying to demonstrate the theoretical principle that at certain times clothes can make a difference. Where do baggy jeans come into play? After admitting that stereotyping about clothing could theoretically be admissible, now we should decide whether it should be admissible in this case.

In a law school classroom setting, I think it is crucial to have theoretically honest discussions. In our attempts to be sensitive we must try not to lose focus of reality. To deny that stereotyping ever exists or is ever justified seemed a bit silly to me, and I hoped that pointing out one extreme example of where it is justified would bring our discussion back on a more honest level. Should it be justified in this case? That question becomes more interesting when we admit that sometimes stereotyping is justified rather than giving a quick answer that it is not justified because it is never justified per se.

After that class news spread around campus that someone was stating that inner city youth were equivalent to KKK members. That bothered me not only because that was not what I was arguing, but also because at that particular day the classroom became a grounds for division rather than for intellectual discussion. I understand that at that particular time, a few days after the Boalt campus walkout and after student activists were arrested, tensions must have been extremely high. Perhaps, I should have been more sensitive in the manner in which I phrased my comment. Yet, I do not regret making such a comment.

Law school must be a forum for open discussion. If issues aren't dealt with honestly in the comfortable philosophical setting of a classroom, then where can they be? The classroom environment is the quintessential place for the exchange of ideas. With so many bright people in such a limited space, it is a shame not to learn from each other. Part of that learning process is challenging what is said. Ideas should be questioned. Policy arguments by professors and students should be debated. That debate and that challenge should come from every angle. When a ridiculous common-law rule injures a certain group of people, I hope that students (particularly from the Left) challenge it. If a counterproposal recommends a solution that would put the expense of alleviating societal ills on the shoulders of another group, I hope students (particularly from the Right) challenge it. Even if we completely disagree with certain ideas set forth by our peers, we still gain from hearing them. In *Abrams* v. *U.S.,* 250 U.S. 616, 630 (1919), Justice Holmes, in supporting free speech, argued: "That the best test of truth is the power of the thought to get itself accepted in the competition of the market, and that truth is the only ground upon which their wishes safely can be carried out." When the classroom is silenced, when anyone feels uncomfortable to speak, we all lose.

In my module, in particular, there exists a great deal of unease between the Right and the Left. I sympathize with the Left much more often. Yet, that does not imply that I won't make comments that I regard as theoretically true when an argument on the Left is weak. Hindering speech and refraining from making logical points only works to all our detriment. In addition, it is important that students on both sides do not sneer or mock other students. The class is harmed when people blacklist others in the classroom discussions. It is obnoxious that when certain people raise their hands, other students immediately raise their hands to counteract what that one person said. Moreover, it is rude when a student is not allowed to use certain words because other students can't imagine he would be looking after the interest of certain groups. At the same time, it is also important that students don't abuse their forum and waste time when they speak.

Again, usually I do not feel inhibited from speaking my mind, but certainly there are uncomfortable times. Most of the time Boalt is a good forum for discussion. There are many people with diverse viewpoints from whom I learn a great deal. Unfortunately, I think classroom discussion is hindered when certain ideas are not allowed to be expressed.

What Ever Happened to John Stuart Mill?

By Nick-Anthony Buford

Law school is perhaps the greatest invention ever devised for taking individual creativity and free thought and locking it up in a box. Here's the idea of law school: Get a liberal arts undergraduate education. Read Kant. Read Locke. Read Emerson. Read Frost. Read Thoreau. Debate the meaning of life, and liberty, and culture. Travel to far away places. Study abroad. Immerse yourself in new friendships and experiences. Grow. Drink. Think broadly about the meaning of something you love, and enjoy. Get an education that personally fits you, and your interests.

Then stop. And throw it all away, and get a McLaw Degree – one size fits all. One opinion fits all. Or so it seems at Berkeley.

You see, at Boalt, or at least to the vocal liberal thought-police of students that think that they must police the law school for signs of intellectual heresy and conservatism, the only thing that the great lawyers do of value is push the envelope of civil liberties law. Contrary thought is not encouraged. Oneness is the rule.

Let's consider the lawfulness of homosexuality for example. Whereas sodomy is a crime in many places, a large number of students at Boalt evidently think that homosexuality is, or should be, constitutionally protected as a part of one's personal privacy. They have a right to think so. But precisely because everyone is clearly entitled to their own opinions, and expressing them publicly, the viewpoint of the students at Boalt who have been agitating publicly for homosexual rights can't be considered to be the only viewpoint on the issue of homosexuality that should be respected. Gay rights is, after all, an issue over which reasonable people differ, sometimes heatedly. Perhaps homosexuals should be granted special legal protection in a number of areas. Or perhaps homosexual activity should not be protected at all, whether on constitutional grounds or to protect the superior interest represented by the traditional family. Or perhaps something in between is right. To say the least, a settled rule of law is unclear here; consensus is elusive. But what I think is clear is that, though loud, the raised voices in favor of homosexual rights at Boalt have chilled contrary speech through intolerance of contrary views.

Where could the law possibly go on this issue? Well, existing trends could continue. It's not unforeseeable, given recent judicial decisions, that in the future the utterance of an opinion contrary to the majority opinion at Boalt in favor of gay rights might be treated as the equivalent of racist hate speech. Or perhaps any meaningful public discussion about whether the dominant opinion on gay rights is the correct one would be treated as creating a hostile work environment in violation of sexual harassment laws. Regardless of the future, the present situation is that already, at Boalt Hall, students who individually challenge the dominant paradigm with their own thoughts are ostracized by many other students at the law school – perhaps intentionally, perhaps unintentionally.

Though I have kept to myself my true feelings about the gay rights movement while at Boalt (talk about racial quotas is the topic *du jour*, it seems), I have felt ostracized nonetheless when I have chosen to express my opinion on other topics. And that shunning has been a direct result of what I have chosen to say in class: about when criminals should be held responsible for their actions; about affirmative action; about taxes; about environmental over-regulation; about property rights being just that – rights; about the proper size and scope of government; and about law. And there are some folks that have managed never to say a word to me – or to say very little to me – all year. In a class of 273, however, that is kind of hard.

I suppose that that ostracization is self-imposed, in the sense that it results from my own voluntary behavior in choosing to express my views. But it is also the result of others – others who are perhaps oversensitive, perhaps petty, or who perhaps just cannot see that all coins have two sides. In my experience, other people at Boalt choose to penalize you when you speak up, by choosing to ostracize you. And at Berkeley – once the great home of the "free speech movement" – that is an odd result I did not expect. My undergraduate institution was full of opinionated people – just like Boalt, but unlike Boalt, the disagreements were not taken personally. In other words, even opinionated people recognized the right of other people to have contrary opinions. At the California Legislature, where I worked for a year as a staff member, there were many disagreements, but by and large the disagreements were not taken personally there either. At Boalt, however, disagreements appear far too frequently to be taken personally. If you don't agree with the dominant liberal strain of thought at Boalt, you *must* be a fascist. I know, for I have heard this label used to describe me at Boalt. Funny, I've always thought of myself as a classic liberal – the type that defends vociferously the rights of people to disagree with me, and to say so, even if I think them to be wrong.

Once, at a reception of some sort, I was asked by a student of color whether, in spite of all the "agitating" at Boalt against the ethnic composition of the mostly white Class of 2000, I felt welcome at the law school as a member of that class? I didn't know what to say, because I hadn't expected the "I take things personally attitude" of other people at Boalt. I forced the answer "yes," but I meant "no." I didn't see the point in trying to explain everything that I felt about how this student's agitating compatriots had made me feel to someone whom I perceived was making a tokenist effort in talking to me. I am a minority. That didn't make me agree that everyone with brown or black or yellow skin must think alike. If that point wasn't self-evident, I didn't see how I could communicate that to someone who didn't already understand it.

It's undeniable that at Boalt, free speech and free discussion are chilled. It affects all of us. And, ironically, the inspiring, "traditional" 1960's paradigm of Berkeley – of respect for diverse opinions – is subverted and trampled by the new intolerance of the activist student thought-police who police the discussions which take place daily in the classrooms and hallways. I remember one instance in particular when I was practically reprimanded by a fellow student for having spoken my mind. It struck me that this verbal, public, high-minded scolding – it was like being put in a New England-style pillory of sorts – implied several things: (1) that this is our turf, and you're not one of us; (2) that on our turf, you'd better play by our rules; and (3) our rule is to allow you only to say that which we can tolerate, so fall in line. Unfortunately, for any self-appointed censors, however, I've decided one thing for certain – whatever it is that bothers others about what I say, I don't plan on stopping. I won't fall in line. It is my prerogative to express myself.

Were he alive today, John Stuart Mill, a libertarian, would not like the Berkeley of today, because he valued freedom of expression and public debate as a method of arriving at fundamental truth. Were he alive today, Henry David Thoreau, a transcendentalist, would not like the Boalt of today, because he appreciated that the freedom to express unpopular views without retribution (the freedom to dissent, in other words) lies at the core of a free society.

But the late Rev. Martin Luther King, Jr., were he alive today, would in fact like Boalt, because today, post affirmative action, he would behold a truly color-blind admissions policy which does justice to the dignity of individuals in the Kantian sense – the dignity that results from not treating people as means to an end, but as morally significant entities in and of themselves.

Speak out loud at Boalt that last thought about Martin Luther King and quotas and Kant, and you will be ostracized, as I have been. You will be ostracized because the thought-police at Boalt can't grasp the importance of the preceding two truths – about the value of public discussion – represented by Mill and Thoreau. One does not truly have the freedom to think, and grow, however, if one cannot express one's thoughts without fear of retribution.

American culture glorifies the dissenting individual. That is in part a direct consequence of Berkeley's 1960's legacy, the counterculture of that era, and the Free Speech Movement that was its genesis. We value the road less traveled by when two paths diverge in a wood. We glorify the person who marches to the beat of a different drum. We value those who have done things their way. Perhaps Boalt will learn this valuable cultural lesson one day (after all, it once taught it) and stop ostracizing dissenting individuals. Until then, I will continue to be the back-bench dissenter in the classroom. I will continue to help expose the dominant paradigm for being what it is – just one way of seeing the world.

In spite of the smothering political correctness at Boalt, I highly recommend it to anyone who likes to think for oneself. The hostility of the "audience" at Boalt to hearing your message can oftentimes be formidable. But press on. It's worth it. There is, after all, no better place to preach the Gospel than in the den of the devil. You see, it is the very hostility of the audience at Boalt that makes your own personal viewpoint that much more worth expressing.

There are so many of us in law school each day, but how many are actually heard from? Not many. I ask you, is that the idea of an education? Is that the idea of law school? It shouldn't be, but it is the idea at Boalt.

Two Jews, a Cuban, and an Indian:
A True Story
By David Wienir

A true story. Two Jews, a Cuban, and an Indian were walking down the street, on their way to law school. Despite the fact that the four students had only been in law school for two weeks and had come from such different ethnic backgrounds, they felt comfortable with each other. One placid fall afternoon, the four new law students began talking, and their conversation went roughly as follows. One of the Jews declared: "I have been here two weeks already, and so far, I have not found an appropriate woman to ask out on a date. It's killing me!" The Indian appeared to catch his reflection in a car window. The Jew added: "Man, who could figure such attractive guys like us would be so lonely in a law school where men are in the minority? Our class is fifty-one percent women!" The Jew stumbled slightly, then continued: "No one understands us. I just came from the activity fair – women's groups, black groups, Latino groups, tree-hugging groups, gay-hugging groups, but no heterosexual male support groups. That would be fine if we didn't need it. But damn it, we have issues, too. Big issues!" The situation seemed impossible.

The Cuban had the solution. He had heard that once upon a time the Boalt Hall School of Law had something like a fraternity, dedicated to discussing men's issues and serving as a support group for average (today read: heterosexual) guys. In addition, the group held social mixers with sophisticated undergraduate Berkeley women. Why did they do this? You see, there was a myth that lawyers should not marry lawyers. No diversity. Bad *karma*.

By creating a fraternity at Boalt Hall, bad *karma* could be avoided, and both of the group's problems could be solved – support for heterosexual men at Boalt, and an opportunity to interact with a large number of interesting, eligible women. The four students were finally happy. Boalt could be a place for them, too.

They all had senses of humor, of course. And one way to confront isolation is humor. The four just wanted to find a way to have a social life – something too many law students go without. They walked into class, and decided – what the heck – to share their idea. The fraternity, one of them declared with self-deprecating humor, would be called "The Fraternal Order of Boalt." Its purpose was simple – to serve as a necessary outlet for heterosexual men (now an "underrepresented" minority?) at the law school, and to meet interesting sorority women. That said, as much as the four were concerned about men's issues, they were interested in having anyone interested participate. The four made it absolutely clear that the fraternity would be open to all Boalt students, regardless of their gender, sexual orientation, and ethnic background. This was stated in plain and clear language. (The idea did not at all seem strange to me, or inappropriate. As an undergraduate at Columbia, I myself was a member of a co-ed fraternity: Alpha Delta Phi.)

What were the four of them doing? Why were they so eager to share their interests? Why not? It didn't seem like a big deal.

Now, here's the punch line. Within the week, I was told that the dean of the law school was notified that something like a white supremacist group had been started at Boalt. Ironically, it appeared to have been founded by two Jews, a Cuban, and an Indian.

Not funny, right? Now, here's the point. As a result of these completely erroneous and unfair allegations, a large portion of my first semester of law school was spent exculpating myself from slanderous claims. I overheard students I had never met discuss the "white supremacist" clan, often mentioning my name. Students I had never even seen before angrily approached me, demanding both explanation and repentance. I increasingly felt uncomfortable walking the halls of my very own law school. Having dedicated the last two years of my life to the British Labour Party, it seemed ironic that I had suddenly come to represent all that was evil in the rich-straight-white-male-dominated world.

I ask any student who spread such rumors: Do you understand what it is like to be called these names when you are a Jew? Do you understand what it is like to be called a racist or a white supremacist when you have spent the last six months working for the Survivors of the Shoah Visual History Foundation, watching endless testimony of Holocaust survivors, with tears flowing down your cheeks? Do you understand what it is like for two Jews, a Cuban, and an Indian to be accused – so recklessly – of being white supremacists? I do.

Names largely stick – my case is no exception. Almost a year after the incident, my name is still being linked to a white-supremacy movement that, to my knowledge, does not, thank God, even exist. To say this hurts is an understatement.

I ask any student who spread such rumors: What have I done to deserve such treatment? Whom have I wronged? Why are you so threatened by the plans of four minority students who simply wish to spend time together talking and meeting women? I cannot speak on behalf of the other Jew, the Cuban, and the Indian, but I ask one question: why is it the case that I, as a straight white male, must not have a room of my own?

CHAPTER FIVE

AN INSTITUTIONALIZED PROBLEM?

Is the threat to free speech an institutionalized problem at UC Berkeley? Perhaps. Just what is an "institutionalized" problem? An institutionalized problem is one that emanates from a tacit or expressed assumption that things are and ought to be a certain way at an institution, whether those assumptions are a matter of official policy or not.

Disorientation Day

By Jeff Bishop

For the most part, I have not found Boalt to be the repressive, Orwellian, ultra-leftist hotbed of activist intimidation that some make it out to be. One recurring exception, however, arises whenever the topic shifts to Proposition 209, or anything else having to do with racial preferences or race relations.

Things flared up in the spring when the 1997 law school admission figures were released. Dean Kay had already taken her share of heat for supporting racial preferences, and was now being criticized for obeying the same law that she had staunchly opposed. Far fewer minorities had been admitted than in previous years, and there was concern that even those admitted might choose to go elsewhere.

And go elsewhere they did. Many, of course, chose schools with reputations better than ours (Yale, Harvard, perhaps Stanford). Others may have had generous scholarships, geographical ties to other regions, or other personal reasons that were beyond our control. Still, I can't help but think that some may have been scared off by well-intentioned, pro-affirmative-action hyperbole.

To the best of my knowledge, Boalt has no chapter of the American Nazi Party, the Aryan Nation, the Klan, or any other hate group. No one cheered when we learned of the decline in minority enrollment. Yet on Admitted Student Day, visitors were treated to dozens of posters urging us to "stop the hate" and asking loaded questions such as "Why do you fear me?" Other posters referred to the "Klan approved" state initiative, welcomed students to "Jim Crow University," and displayed names and silhouettes of practically every past minority applicant who had not been hired for a faculty position. Students wore red armbands reminiscent of East Germany. A crowd gathered like a lynch mob, cheering while one destroyed a piñata named "diversity." Several first-year law students noted that had they seen such a spectacle the year before, they would not have attended Boalt.

No one can deny that smear campaigns are often effective. A television advertisement with a mushroom cloud got Lyndon Johnson elected President as a peace candidate. Negative campaigning probably weakened Proposition 209's support considerably as well. But mudslinging carries a very high price tag. It destroys open and honest debate, and ultimately soils the entire process rather than just the intended target.

There is simply no way to admonish the Boalt community to "stop the hate" without sending a not-so-subtle message that the Boalt community has a good deal of hate which needs stopping. We aren't a hateful group at all, but I can hardly blame any potential minority student who attended last year's orientation and concluded otherwise.

An Institutionalized Problem

By Richard Kevin Welsh

PART ONE: THE PREVAILING DOGMA

Boalt Hall has frustrated intellectual discourse by fostering an environment in which too many subjects remain taboo and too many perspectives are silenced. This phenomenon cannot be blamed on one man or one mob; rather it is institutionalized, systematically perpetuating the school's prevailing ethos. It is unseen, but present. It attacks arrogance, but radiates it. It disdains stereotypes, but employs them. It despises traditional conformity, but promotes an oppressive, uniform brand of dogmatic egalitarianism. It advances a morality bewilderingly egocentric and all-embracing. It taps into the most cynical veins of human emotion, engendering a fanatical and inflexible ideology that serves as a wellspring for a bottomless reservoir of hate, from which the institution derives its energy.

Boalt refuses to tolerate. It enervates, levels, and breaks, until people resign and embrace its collectivist discipline. Under the guise of personal freedom yet always championing individual equality, Boalt wrests away all that is individual from the individual, casting him off either to advance its ideologies or leaving him with nothing. And, if necessary, it sacrifices the enduring iconoclast at the altar of equality. No prejudice survives Boalt's reductionism – though its curriculum largely comports with traditional legal teachings which emphasize precedent. Boalt attacks both students and visitors with equal fervor, impugning whoever or whatever fails to bow to its epicurean gods.[1]

Having served four years as a noncommissioned officer in the United States Army Airborne Rangers, I think particularly deplorable the manner in which military recruiters are treated when they seek to enlist Boalt students into the armed services. The men and women of the armed forces are called upon to make tremendous sacrifices, for which the vast majority Americans express their utmost gratitude. When these service members visit Boalt Hall, however, they are greeted by a mob of wild-eyed radicals, who inveigh against the military with the tacit if not express approval of the school's hierarchy. The halls at Boalt are peppered with anti-military propaganda (probably paid for with taxpayer money), largely bemoaning the military policies that prohibit open homosexuality and forbid women to partake in most combat arms.

The Boalt administration suggests that it would ban the military, but for the grant money the university receives from the federal government (a cost-benefit analysis that flies in the face of its so-called principles). Though the Boalt faculty and student body are utterly ignorant about military management; they attack the policies under which the armed forces operate largely because these fail *their* test of equality. Boalt fails to recognize that the armed forces are manned by real people, with real prejudices, who must obey orders in chaotic situations, irrespective of their idiosyncratic desires.

Undermining traditional morality in academia is one thing, but exploding the foundation which supports our edifice of freedom is another. This is not to argue that faculty and students should not protest against policies they think immoral. I think it ironic, however, that Boalt expresses an *unqualified* disdain for the very institution under which the school's ability to act freely has been protected. Rather than hector military personnel, Boalt should thank them. Neither gratitude nor empathy have a place in radical ideology, however, for it operates without concern for circumstance, tradition, or reality.

---

[1] One can hardly imagine that Boalt Hall would appoint a conservative as the school's dean.

Boalt, too, tramples underfoot any student who stands in its path. Reacting to a remark made by Ward Connerly in which he suggested that white law students would not relinquish their seats to support affirmative action, the student radicals set out to show that they were indeed willing to act (theatrically, at least, for if the white liberal were truly required to abandon his seat, I think Regent Connerly's prediction would prove correct). In Professor John Diamond's Torts class, several white students abandoned their seats, enabling "students of color" (as defined by the one-drop rule) to share "their experiences" with the class.[2] The student radicals even launched a personal attack against Professor Diamond himself – though he made it quite apparent throughout the semester that he also embraces radical ideologies. Dean Herma Hill Kay, an avowed supporter of racial preferences, attempted to prevent unregistered students, among others, from ruining Professor Diamond's lecture. Dean Kay's efforts, however, are most aptly described as half-hearted at best.[3]

Once the radicals captured the classroom, they began to ask questions which were wholly unrelated to the topic of the lecture.

---

[2] This essay is not the place to debunk this theory.

[3] Given the way in which Dean Kay has pandered to the student Left, and the way she has brazenly attempted to circumvent the will of the people of California with respect to Proposition 209, I think it arguable that she failed to call upon adequate support to prevent the student radicals from ruining Professor Diamond's lecture because she approves of their cause *and* their conduct.

In contrast, on April 3, 1998, Dean Kay circulated a memorandum in which she noted that someone had defaced a student organization bulletin board. In this memo, she suggested that "[w]e must all be committed to protecting the freedom of our students and our student groups and to fostering an atmosphere of mutual respect in which intelligent discourse will prevail over efforts to exclude some voices from the debate." Dean Kay failed to inform the students that it was the Federalist Society's bulletin board that was defaced, thus suggesting that she lacks the fortitude to defend outright the organization's right to express its views. [*Editors' Note:* See Appendices B and C.]

Further, Dean Kay perpetuates a monolithic façade, which can be quite vexing to dissenting students at Boalt. For example, on May 6, 1998, she issued a mem-orandum in which she noted "[w]e got some good press today about our admission numbers." She stapled therewith several newspaper clippings noting that Boalt's

After giving a prefabricated speech in which they claimed their voices were unheard, most (but not all) of the fire-breathing radicals then exited the classroom mid-lecture, chanting some incoherent incantation designed to disrupt the class and demonstrate to the press that they were serious. These students were unconcerned about the interests of the students with whom they lack common political aspirations, that is, with the students who find torts interesting and political radicalism uninteresting. The collectivist morality always sacrifices the individual to the multitude, for means bear little weight *vis-a-vis* ends in its calculus.

I could write endlessly about Boalt's hypocrisies, but I am too young (or cowardly) a candidate for martyrdom. The intellectually honest, however, doubtless know that I advance the truth. Boalt Hall has no true friends, only true enemies. Its venom poisons the unready mind, seizing one's ability to question clearly the institution's prevailing dogma – a dogma that thrashes the human spirit. At bottom, the students and faculty are *perhaps* tolerant, but Boalt Hall is not.

---

minority enrollment has improved, because the school now places less value on the traditional objective factors such as the grade point average and the Law School Admission Test. Though it improved minority representation, Boalt Hall's subterfuge was not "good press" to students who believe that race lacks a valuable relationship to the concept of merit.

Moreover, Dean Kay failed to note in her memorandum the ten percent fall in male admission offers, representing a drop in male representation to well under fifty percent of the class — part of Dean Kay's "good press," no doubt. Like the student radicals, Dean Kay employs result-oriented reasoning and cares little about the feelings of the students who hold minority philosophical positions at Boalt. I do not, however, identify myself based on my sex, sexuality, or race, so my psychological frame remains largely undamaged. The extent to which people identify themselves by sex, sexuality, or race is a sign of personal weakness, for these categories provide nothing but an unstable crutch upon which to support the forlorn egalitarian's frail self-esteem and self-identity.

In my essay "The Prevailing Dogma," I employed language that a Boalt Hall outsider may consider hyperbolic, or perhaps even evidence of paranoia. I suggested that Boalt Hall sacrifices "the enduring iconoclast," that the institution "tramples underfoot any student who stands in its path." Yet I failed to offer the reader a truly egregious anecdote. Several months after I submitted my essay to David Wienir, I was accused of cheating during a power blackout in my first-year Contracts exam by the student body's president-elect, a left-wing activist (hereinafter, "the accuser") who has dedicated his energy to promoting "social justice." I write this essay reluctantly, because I find the subject matter embarrassing and difficult to incorporate into a short, yet comprehensive, essay. Further, I am currently pursuing an outside appeal with the university's ombudsman, because I have exhaustively traveled the jagged avenues of recourse offered by the law school. This update will, however, provide the reader with a truly egregious anecdote. In short, it will illuminate the politics of Boalt Hall. I will first briefly address the facts surrounding the accusation. Then, I will focus on the administration's subsequent conduct and how it has affected my family's well-being.

This tale of institutional ineptitude and viciousness begins on May 19, 1998, when the power failed with approximately twelve minutes left in my Contracts exam, throwing the windowless classroom into *total* darkness. The proctors reentered and told the students to leave their belongings and exit. Approximately forty-five minutes later, an administrator told some fellow students and me that the power would be restored and that, in accordance with the school's policy, we would be allowed to finish the exam. About fifteen minutes later, however, the administration decided to terminate the exam, allegedly issuing an order that the test would be collected. Like several other students who have testified on my behalf, I did not hear this order. In fact, the events that ensued show that clear orders were *not* issued.

When reentry began, I was outside (with several other students) and saw people rushing into the classroom. My adrenaline pumping, I rushed inside with the belief that the power had been restored. Two proctors holding flashlights, however, were stationed at the bottom of the stairs so as to safely guide the students through the dark room to their seats. The proctor's flashlight provided enough light to enable me to see many students writing, some organizing, and others sitting tight. Several students asked the proctors for information, but they were largely reticent, thereby provoking angry demands for coherent marching orders (as any lawyer will attest, first-year law school exams are very stressful, even if everything goes smoothly). Amidst this chaos, I sat down, numbered my bluebooks, and began to try to organize my work in case the power was restored.

At this point, the accuser, peering over my left shoulder, then trumpeted: "Rick!, that's so extremely dishonest! That's so extremely dishonest, Rick! That's so disrespectful, Rick!" I was shocked, pushed my papers away, and placed my pen in my backpack. Facing public humiliation, I asked the accuser to keep his thoughts to himself or between the two of us. He made another loud utterance which was incomprehensible, though it certainly drew more people's attention. I again asked him to please keep his thoughts to himself, at which point he told me not to worry because he would not tell anyone.[4] About two minutes later, a senior administrator entered the classroom and, in a manner wrought with frustration, ordered us not to write *anything* at all – the bright line had finally been drawn. The tests were then collected.

In class, I successfully subdued the accuser, but, as I gave the situation more thought, I believed that he might seize this opportuni-

---

[4] According to the assistant dean, the accuser told her about my alleged Honor Code violation soon after the exam terminated, which suggests that the accuser never intended on keeping his thoughts to himself. I think that he simply wanted to speak to the administration first. The assistant dean failed to inform me of the accusation until the next evening and then only in vague terms. Had I thought private reconciliation impossible, I would have approached the dean immediately and taken my chances with her. At this point, I had yet to complete my exams. After implying that she believed the accuser, the assistant dean wished me "good luck" on my final exam.

ty to besmirch my name and possibly have me expelled.[5] Why? I have publicly criticized policies that the accuser has striven to advance. In the *San Francisco Chronicle*, for example, I characterized the student leaders at Boalt as "contemptible," a remark that drew the accuser's ire. This article was pinned to several bulletin boards in Boalt Hall, thereby making me *persona non grata*. Further, the accuser and I shared the same first-year seminar and, inasmuch as possible, debated bitterly. Lastly, the accuser also has a history of publicly condemning me. In the fall, for instance, he humiliated me at a signature drive for an initiative which would eliminate Proposition 209, the California constitutional amendment which forbids, among other things, racial preferences. Because he serves as Boalt Hall's chief student representative (wheras I am one of its chief critics), I knew that the accuser would be a particularly emphatic and believable witness. Boalt Hall is arguably the nation's most politi-cized law school and periodically manifests a willingness to infringe the rights or harm the reputations of anyone (recall Professor Diamond's treatment) with whom it lacks common political goals. I thus sought to placate the accuser by seeking private reconciliation via e-mail, but my efforts proved to be a futile attempt to tap a com-passionate vein.

On May 20, the assistant dean informed me that I had been accused of violating Boalt Hall's Honor Code. I told her that I knew the accuser's identity and that I had communicated with him, but she refused to confirm my statement.[6] I immediately wrote the assis-tant dean an extensive, detailed statement, which cut into my time to finish my last paper and severely shook my piece of mind. In my statement, I informed the assistant dean that my wedding was three weeks away and that I wanted to finish any investigation beforehand. She said that the administration would seek a "speedy resolution."

---

[5] As elucidated in "The Prevailing Dogma," the student Left and the administration has manifested a willingness to employ tactics that harm individual rights and rep-utations, which alone explains my reluctance to approach the administration after the accuser trumpeted his vague accusations.

[6] Apparently, the accuser's anonymity outweighed my right to obtain fresh testimony and refute his account.

However, I waited almost two months before a hearing date was set, during which time the specter of this career-threatening investigation haunted my wedding, honeymoon, and Independence Day celebration. My wife asked for a situation report almost daily, but, though I pursued the assistant dean diligently, I lacked any information with which to keep her abreast. The administration never stated the potential range of sanctions, and, because I thought it might suggest guilt, I was afraid to ask. My wife and I were uncertain as to what the future might hold – left in limbo, so to speak – a mental state that severely dampened our summer.

The assistant dean eventually set the oral hearing for July 7, at which time I received the accuser's written statement. The statement was very brief, but obviously embellished. It stated that, in response to the accuser's allegations, "all" I said was: "I know." In his written statement, the accuser claimed he was one of the *first* students to reenter the classroom, at which point he saw me "writing furiously" in my bluebook.[7] In his oral testimony, however, he said that he was outside and entered last. At the oral hearing, the Honor Code Board never challenged the accuser's inconsistent testimony and it was clear that, despite the phony courtesy with which I was treated, every presumption would militate against me. I had consistently maintained that I was one of the last people to reenter the class, but, because I was not given the accuser's statement, I never knew that his testimony would survive or falter based on my ability to corroborate my original statement. In short, I consistently claimed that the accuser approached me from my seven o'clock, which, because his seat was behind mine, would be consistent with his written and most accurate statement.[8] Had I read the accuser's statement immediately after the exam, I most probably could have obtained testimony to support the fact that I entered last. Standing at my seven o'clock, the accuser lacked a clear

---

[7] Rumor has it that I stayed or sneaked back in the classroom after the students originally exited.

[8] At the oral hearing, the accuser, when asked an unrelated question, stated that his written statement was his most accurate account.

view of my right hand.[9]   In conclusion, I was given two days to submit any additional information. I wrote a short rebuttal, in which I illuminated the accuser's inconsistent and exaggerated testimony. I thought that the accuser's inconsistencies, actions, and other mitigating factors (e.g., the darkness) would create more than enough doubt to win my case. However, I soon realized that, unless the accuser retracted his statement, anything I tried would prove futile.

Largely because I e-mailed the accuser seeking private reconciliation, the Honor Code Board accepted the accuser's characterizations of my actions, simply stating that, though I probably gained no advantage over my fellow students, I must have done "at least some" substantive writing in my bluebook. The Board's official letter, which I received on July 28, confirmed my worst beliefs, for it failed to mention that the accuser and I had a history of public antipathy or the accuser's inconsistent testimony. I understand that the administration does not want to politicize Boalt's Honor Code, but, given these circumstances, I think it absurd that the Board found this history and consistency irrelevant. These are strong grounds on which to impeach a witness. Further, the official letter contains "admissions" accredited to me which I *never* made, such as that the accuser and I agreed that he told me to stop writing. Though I think that I clearly showed that the inconsistent testimony of one partisan eyewitness was insufficient grounds upon which to base an Honor Code violation, the Board apparently rejected my testimony as to motives for seeking private reconciliation and grounded its finding thereon. In the best light, the Board apparently thought that my mistrust of the administration was groundless. As I portended, however, the Honor Code process was unjust: I was given no opportunity to prepare for my oral hearing, making it difficult to chart a prudent course of action because I could not attack the accuser's testimony or corroborate key facts in my statement.

---

[9]   Further, a proctor was standing at my twelve o'clock not more than ten feet away, unimpeded by any obstruction whatsoever. The proctor had a flashlight, but he never saw me "writing furiously."

I appealed the Board's finding to Dean Herma Hill Kay, but she wrote that the Board had considered "all of the relevant facts" and had done the "best job possible." The Board's decision, however, was based on the unfettered intuition of four academics and the inconsistent testimony of a bitter partisan. I had a twenty-minute, "informal" oral hearing that was conducted two months after the exam, at which I received my accuser's statement for the first time. A material fact relating to his location as an eyewitness was contained in this belated information. But I had no opportunity to confront the accuser and force him to address his inconsistencies. At the same time, I was bombarded with questions by the Board, to which I responded consistently. Further, I asked Dean Kay to note the accuser's changed testimony and disdain for conservatives and to correct the out-and-out inaccuracies contained in the official report. The report also failed to note that I was sitting directly in front of the proctor. These facts are obviously germane.

Without *any* substantive explanation, however, Dean Kay rejected my lengthy appeal outright, but reiterated that, barring a "future violation," the Board's letter would *not* be disclosed to *anyone* and that it would *not* be placed in my permanent file. She also stated that I could appeal to the university's ombudsman. I inquired about the efficacy of the appeals process, but Dean Kay would not tell me whether or not *any* person in Boalt's history has ever won an appeal outside the law school. She cited student "confidentiality," though I never asked for anything but a simple yes or no answer to my query. Further, she refused to state whether or not I was the only student accused of writing during the Contracts exam – a fact that would help show bias, since other students testified that they, too, saw students writing.

Though I could have immured my story within the walls of Boalt Hall, I think it important that I *disclose* the nature and outcome of my Honor Code hearing, because it illuminates the brutish politics that the Left will employ whenever someone challenges its prevailing dogma. Instead of approaching me like a man, the accuser trumpeted vague accusations loudly, which, in my opinion, suggests that he was more interested in blackening my character than in rectifying an academic harm. The administration, moreover, has marched with the accuser from the onset of the investigation. It has tried to preserve the accuser's political viability and protect the school's welfare, while brazenly denying me due process. Nothing else could explain why the official letter refers to the accuser as "the student witness," a term which suggests disinterestedness and preserves his anonymity. Nothing else could explain why the Board failed to note the administrative ineptitude with which the reentry into the classroom was handled, and that, because of this ineptitude, many students were writing.[10] Nothing else could explain why the Board included "admissions" that I never made. In contrast, I face a glut of unfounded rumor, most of which I will never fully debunk.

However, I think that I have illuminated Boalt Hall's twisted paradox: it is a first-rate law school, but it lacks respect for both procedural justice and individual rights. Boalt Hall cares only about outcomes and groups, not about process or individuals. From the ruthless manner of the initial accusation to the unjust and lengthy process of my hearing, I think that I have been treated in a manner that most closely parallels the recently documented, procedural horrors of the Soviet penal system – a system before which individuals stood *equally* worthless, a system that bred scapegoats for its failures and then slaughtered them publicly to intimidate the herd.[11]

---

[10] I do not know if other students wrote in their bluebooks, but I have been told that substantive writing transpired. I think that the accuser's accusation was the only one brought forth, largely because most people thought that the circumstances were too unusual and too chaotic to file a charge for any conduct that transpired before the senior administrator ordered everyone to stop writing.

[11] This analogy is not meant to trivialize the terror under which the citizens of Eastern Europe lived for approximately seventy years.

Boalt's Incentive Programs

Anonymous

Although Boalt's clinical program and loan repayment creates incentives to work for the public interest, Boalt's definition of public interest makes no sense. I wanted to receive school credit for working at the city attorney's office over the summer, but Boalt would not allow it. The theory was that even though my internship would be unpaid and consist of legal work, no credit would be allowed because Boalt does not allow students to receive credit for summer work, even if free.

But for some reason, Boalt gives summer credit for work at Berkeley Community Law Center (BCLC), which has an $800,000/year budget. Boalt favors BCLC so much that it allows BCLC, and BCLC only, to award students for summer work with up to 5 units of credit towards the completion of their law degree. If a student decides to work anywhere else for free, including working with a judge or at an environmental firm, the student cannot receive credit.

Boalt also fosters a program whereby graduates can be relieved from part or all of their law school loans by working for public interest. Although this sounds great in theory, Boalt has an absurd definition of public interest. For example, a job at the public defender's office will count as public interest, but working for the district attorney will not. Why does defending a rapist count as public interest while prosecuting a rapist does not count? Maybe because a public defender's salary is so low that Boalt should compensate. That is not the answer, because doing a low-paying clerkship will not allow a student to receive any loan forgiveness. Boalt's reply: most clerks end up working for firms.

The only reasonable conclusion is that the administration at Boalt has certain preferences, such as working for BCLC and working for the public defender.

CHAPTER SIX

THE DISSENT – "IT'S YOUR PROBLEM"

People who are devoted to a diversity of opinions give all views their sincere attention. The writers printed here suggest that there are no significant threats to intellectual diversity at Boalt Hall. The burden to speak freely, they argue, lies squarely on the shoulders of those who feel silenced.

Stop All the Whining
By Lesley R. Knapp

Maybe I'm just oblivious to the whole thing, but I don't understand why people feel like there isn't a forum for free exchange of ideas here at Boalt. I have never felt intimidated to speak by other people. If people laugh at me, scoff at me, hate me, so be it.

I'm of the opinion that if you want to say something, say it. If you let other people intimidate you or shut you up, that's your problem. I know, I know, that sounds really harsh. But at this point in your life, having been through years of formal education plus some modicum of real-life experience, if you haven't learned to speak up for your own ideas, what have you been doing? Granted, shyness and fear of public speaking can quiet a person, but notice that those are internal controls on your voice and not something external that needs to be remedied or bitched about.

Everywhere people are going to try to talk over you, put you down, keep you quiet. If you're expecting everyone to listen as intently and receptively as a paid therapist, you will continue to be sadly disappointed and frustrated. If you want your ideas heard, speak them and speak them loudly enough. One of my favorite professors once said, "If you're gonna make a mistake, make it a big loud one." Now, I'm not advocating being a public idiot, but why be afraid? The worst anybody can do is laugh at you and whisper some petty nasty little snip to their neighbor.

If you can't speak up for yourself, how are you going to be able to speak up for your clients, constituents, or whoever else might need your voice? Look where you are, what you're doing, what you want to become. Life isn't going to stop politely to listen to a frail little voice, even if it should. Law school, even a pretty friendly one like Boalt, is a challenging place to practice using your voice if you have failed to put it to use before now. You're going to have to fight to be heard everywhere; if you're not willing to fight, quit whining and go revel in your own selfish, self-imposed silence.

Quibbles about the Margins
By Joshua Rider

My initial reaction to being asked to contribute to a collection of thoughts on the state of free discussion at Boalt was hesitant. While I looked forward to reading such a collection, I felt that I had little to say that would be of interest, as my opinions on this issue are neither particularly passionate, nor to my mind, exceptional among my classmates. If anything, I feel I am more staid than many of my classmates. I am a bit older than the average – perhaps my fire for such things is somewhat abated.

Still, the inviter was a friend, and swayed me with the desire to make the collection as broadly representative as possible after going so far as to remind me of the need for even the mediocre to have representation. Persuaded by this and by his chiding that a diary-like tone was not only allowed but expected, I reluctantly agreed. I hope the result is neither too obvious nor too boring to delay the reader from the rest of the tome.

The question before me is: "How open and free is the flow of opinion at Boalt?" To which my immediate and considered answer is borrowed from my Constitutional Law professor, his all-too-familiar refrain of "compared to what?" Is the Boalt community as tolerant of dissenting voices and opinions as one might ideally desire? Surely not. Is it as bad as anywhere else? Has this important center of the Free Speech Movement paradoxically become a place where little is tolerated except lock step conformity? Hardly.

Boalt strikes me as freer and more tolerant than I expected of a law school (even the law school at Berkeley), in most ways, and less so in but a few. I was particularly struck my first semester by how genuinely curious and open-minded most of my classmates seemed – how willing they were to consider alternative viewpoints both in the classroom and out. Far different from the enervated preprofessionalism I had been warned of and had prepared for, at even the best of law schools.

Surely there were exceptions, students that seemed strident in pushing a point upon both professors and classmates, and less than gracious with disagreement, but they were just that: exceptions.

Admittedly, things have changed a bit as we have gone through the first year. Some of the tolerance and civility of the first days seems to have been generated by the uncertainty of new environs, and the lingering possibility that we might not succeed here as we had done before. This wore off. The process accelerated after the first-semester grades were released. Most students found that if they didn't do as well as they wished, they certainly weren't in danger of being run off campus.

The second semester has been less civil than the first. While I'm not sure political convictions are any more strongly held than before, they are certainly expressed more openly, and difference of opinion is more likely to be thought of as error. More students tuned out their classmates more readily. More whispered comments, giggles, eye rolls, shoulder shrugs, sneers, etc., during class signal when a comment is unpopular (I admit to being guilty of all this from time to time, although I do try to police myself in such things). Appellations previously absent, like "fascist" and "terrorist," are used by some, if only at the margins or among like-minded spirits. I know not whether this trend will continue or accelerate throughout my stay here, but I think not. The atmosphere has seemed to me to reach a stasis, and we seem no more or less civil to one another than the second- and third-year students I know.

What's the effect of the sort of minor incivility that characterizes our classroom interaction on the real flow of ideas around here? Not much. One thing that accounts for this is that the eye-rolling, shoulder shrugs, and sneers during class seems equally directed toward students who feel the occasional need to voice calls for THE REVOLUTION and those who suggest everything went wrong at the New Deal. Also, most of those who have some real political conviction don't seem to be anything but energized by the reactions they receive. While I'm sure at times the "micro-aggressions" (if I can borrow and probably misuse that evocative term) that characterizes our classroom and extracurricular behavior hurt those who are subject to them, this pain doesn't seem to silence.

There are some exceptional examples of bad behavior: Boalt Hall building walls spray-painted, fire alarms pulled, posters for certain groups pulled down. All I can say to this is that no one is willing to claim responsibility, we're not even sure law students are involved, everyone seems willing to say it's a bad idea, and the targets of such actions naturally blame their political opponents, all of which strikes me as pretty lame. No one here has been beaten, threatened, ostracized, or even seriously snubbed, as far as I can tell, for their political opinions or actions. I don't mean to suggest that an atmosphere is non-representative simply due to the absence of these things, but I do mean to say that democracy does require a thick skin. The incivility at Boalt is just that and nothing more. Being called a racist or a terrorist may not be much fun, but, hey, anyone silenced by this doesn't have much interest in speaking.

If I'm right and the discourse here at Boalt is occasionally puerile but otherwise evenhanded in its civility, why all the complaining? Make no mistake, there is a lot of complaining, as I'm sure some of the other contributions demonstrate. As seems all too common in our larger political discourse, everyone at Boalt is a victim. Everyone is a target for the forces of (take your pick): the liberal bias of established academia/cultural elite, the conservative backlash of the right-of-center, the hopelessly politically correct, or the white, able-bodied, straight, well-to-do males (in the interest of full disclosure: this last is an incomplete but nevertheless accurate description of the author of this submission).

I think the explanation for this is perfectly simple: we are law students, pursuing a career in, arguably, vindication of rights, slights, and yes, social causes. We do not take slights gracefully, it is not in us. We are not selected (or self-selected) for our stoicism. Law is the center of whiners, in the very best sense of the word. Not Woody Allenesque, get-on-the-couch-and-bitch whiners, but the "I-can't-believe-the-world-is-this-screwed-up" whiners. So it does not surprise me when we all seem a little more ready to complain of the injustice of it all than even the mainstream American victim. This explanation may strike one as glib, but I'm convinced it is a large part of the story.

I've spent a lot of time talking about the student body. What about the faculty, staff, administration? I'm not really qualified to hold forth on these things other than to say that I haven't seen or heard a professor silence a viewpoint in the classroom that was even tangentially related to the course of study – with one exception. On about the fourth or fifth day of my first semester, Professor Dwyer informed the 120 first-year students in his property class that, while the view that could be summarized "all property is theft" was perfectly coherent and could be argued cogently, such a view would not allow one to score well on the bar exam. He discouraged, but did not disallow, taking such a view as one's first premise in doing our reading and our writing assignments for the class. He merely reminded us that one would be accountable for the nuances of the rule against perpetuities regardless. He further suggested that if one held that view seriously, one might be at the margins of the law curriculum and might want to think about a joint degree of some kind. This approach seems pretty typical of the faculty I've encountered.

One final observation, put forward even more reluctantly than the rest. There is one kind of silencing that pervades the Boalt discourse: admissions to the community, both for faculty and students. In this Boalt is suffering. The racial/ethnic/economic diversity of my class (and of the classes that preceded me, and certainly of the classes to come during my time here) is not representative of that of the state of California or of the nation. No one is silenced once they get here, it's getting here that's the gag. There are opinions and positions and voices in the American debate that are not heard here. Not because those here don't speak them, but because those who speak them are not here.

I don't know what to say about this. The problem is horrific here, but only marginally less so throughout the rest of elite legal education. The causes run far beyond Boalt. I believe, though I'm willing to be convinced otherwise, that the faculty and administration are not doing everything that could be done to combat the re-segregation of this campus. I believe, though I would hope to be convinced otherwise, that even were they doing everything within their power under the law (and yes somewhat beyond it) the situation would confound them – they simply do not have enough power to cure this. That, of course, does not excuse the insufficiency of the efforts. Similar observations could be made of the diversity of the faculty itself. Given the magnitude and scope of the problem of entrance to this community, the problems of censorship once we're here are quibbles about the margins.

CHAPTER SEVEN

REFLECTIONS ON AFFIRMATIVE ACTION

Without a doubt, the most controversial topic throughout the 1997-98 academic year at UC Berkeley was racial preference in admissions policies. The writers here, with both bravery and feeling, confront not only that topic squarely, but also the repercussions of expressing one's views, or refusing publicly to support the 'diversity' protesters. Unlike the writer of the previous essay, the writers here are unwilling to reduce "problems of censorship" to "quibbles."
Most compelling, though, is their personal perspectives on the requirements of real tolerance and true peace.

Reflections on Proposition 209
By Darcy Edmonds

I used to vacillate on the topic of affirmative action. I support the concept of upholding and increasing diversity in education, business, and government. However, I do not feel that affirmative action, as it existed, was helping, any more than it was harming, the goal of equality. My experiences as a member of Boalt Hall Class of 2000, the first class admitted under Proposition 209, acutely sharpened my awareness of the urgency of the issue and have helped clarify my own position.

I began the year with an optimistic outlook on how Boalt students would cope with the new policy. My first day, however, became a sign of what was to come. Protests, petitions, and news cameras dominated the campus as students loudly voiced their opposition to Proposition 209. I feared confrontation with fellow students asking me to carry signs and demonstrate for a cause about which I was still unsure. I avoided those students who seemed to be the leaders – uncertain of whether my thoughts would be understood if I was surveyed.

As the days passed and classes demanded more attention, the movement faded into the background a little. The tension on campus was still quite real, but it was less controlling of everyday events. Yet, it was not long before a plan arose for a staged "walkout" from classes. All students were invited to participate, and some of the

Caucasian students, including myself, were asked directly to help by giving up our seats during class to students of other ethnicities who were planning to enter during the lecture. I agreed with their intention of showing that the students were united in their belief in diversity in the classroom, so I agreed to participate.

I was not informed that the rest of the plan included repeated disruptions throughout the class period and a personal attack upon the professor for simply trying to carry on with his lecture. The demonstration culminated in loud chanting as the students marched out of the room in protest. As I sat on the steps at the front of the classroom, I was embarrassed to be seen as a supporter of these offensive tactics and felt guilty and regretful in front of the professor. Rather than convincing me of the exigency of the situation, these actions pushed me toward opposing their cause. I was thrilled when a fellow student distributed a letter to all students commenting on the preceding day's events and his frustration with the leaders for using himself and other students like pawns in their game of political strategy. His letter mirrored my own feelings about the previous day's events. Soon after, he was publicly attacked for his comments, convincing me not to make the same mistake he did by voicing my own feelings. I felt I could not tell anyone my personal philosophies – that I wanted to increase opportunities for students of diverse backgrounds but did not support affirmative action.

The year continued with occasional shows of protest, some positive, others negative. One Monday I came to school to find courtyard walls spray-painted with a statement about diversity, another misguided outburst that was destructive rather than curative. I began to speak more candidly with certain friends who affirmed my contentions. They, too, were not willing to risk resentment by voicing their honest opinions.

Boalt students make up an extraordinary mix of ideologies, and I believe that is part of what gives the school its remarkable character and reputation. In fact, the combination of a historically liberal campus and some of the brightest minds in the country, as well as a group of students heading toward high-income careers, is unique to Boalt and part of what makes the school so attractive to prospective students. Further, the clash of these tenets exposes law students to a kind of training essential to legal practice but unobtainable in a classroom. The loss of this forum would be devastating to the essential quality that is Boalt.

These events have led me to a number of conclusions about the situation California and the country are currently facing. I do not agree with perpetuating affirmative action as it has existed; the result has been a new kind of discrimination. I do not agree that reverse discrimination is fair simply because it is "someone else's turn." Affirmative action was only a Band–Aid™ on the problem. The real solution must take place much earlier in the lives of each student. When I reflect upon my own education, I have trouble justifying the fact that my public elementary school, which was located in a rather wealthy community, had computers and small class sizes while the neighboring school in a poor community had difficulty funding even books. This is where the inequality takes effect. By the time students reach the college level, many have already been lost in the system where affirmative action did not reach, not to mention graduate education that, even before Proposition 209, has been dominated by a higher-income student body.

I feel that the goals of affirmative action simply require new means for attaining them. I find it terribly unfortunate that students such as myself have been stifled rather than able to add to the forum of ideas on how to address the problem. I understand that this was not the aim of the students at Boalt, but it is the grievous result.

Not On Campus, Of Course
By Megan Elizabeth Murray

PART ONE: NO SPECIAL HANDSHAKE

An interesting underground society exists at Boalt Hall. It has no secret meetings or special handshake. Unfortunately, its membership is as secret as the Masons was before its recent reform. Even the members themselves do not know each other's identities. It is a society of political conservatives.

I discovered the existence of the group in October of my first year at Boalt. It was the fall semester of 1997, and affirmative action protests were raging. Fire alarms were repeatedly set off, though no one claimed to know anything about them. Propaganda was delivered to our mailboxes every morning. No one in the halls dared to utter a word in opposition to affirmative action. It really bothered me. I did not understand why no one was expressing any other view.

As a new transfer student, I knew very few people. My main resources were third-year students who had transferred to Boalt the previous year. I was speaking to one of them in a secluded hallway when I asked her about the lack of a conservative voice in the school. She told me that she agreed with my views, but that it would not be a good idea to voice them. She even lowered her voice and changed the subject when someone walked by. "He's really liberal," she explained when he had passed.

I told her I was thinking of writing something. I was considering a flyer to post, a pamphlet to distribute in mailboxes, or an article to publish in the *Cross-Examiner*, a student publication at the law school. My classmate warned me not to write. I should not create a stir, she told me.

The more I thought about this conversation the more wounded I felt. If other students agreed with me, or at least held views different from those being publicized, we had a right to engage in public discourse and express those views. Creating stirs being one of my specialties, I wrote the article. I submitted it to the *Cross-Examiner*, believing it would reach a larger audience, including the faculty, through the publication than through posting or mailbox distribution. Unfortunately, due to unforeseen timing issues, it was not published until the following February (1998).* By that time, the furor over affirmative action had become a dull roar, and the lynch mob I expected at my front door did not materialize.

I had truly expected some response to my article. My impression from my classmate had been that there was a group of people who wanted to say the things I wrote in my article, but who simply did not want to be the ones to say them. I thought I would hear from those people. If not them, I at least expected to hear from my opposition. I anticipated attacks on my arguments. I received no response at all. I came to the conclusion that no unseen group of conservative thinkers existed. Even my opposition did not take me seriously enough to respond to me. I felt alone, but also proud that I had spoken for myself.

Later in the spring semester I found out that I was not alone at all. A friend and I were discussing a professor who, when she found that he was more interested in corporate than public interest law, said to another student, "And he looks like such a nice guy," or something with that gist. Our conversation headed toward the lack of respect for opposing views and other manifestations of political bigotry at Boalt.

---

* *Editors' Note*: The article, which was included by the author as part of her submission, is reprinted below as "Part Two."

My friend turned to me and asked, "Didn't you write that article in the *Cross-Ex*?"

"Yes," I nervously replied. I was prepared for a browbeating in February. I was not now.

"Thank you," he said. I was in shock. Could it be that someone shared my view? It could, and it was. My friend confided that I had written things that he had been wanting to say.

"I didn't know anyone had even read it," I told him, referring to the lack of response I had received.

"Oh, they read it, and they talked about it. I know a lot of people who agreed with it, too. Of course, they wouldn't say so on campus." Not on campus. Of course. What was I thinking expecting a mature public discussion in a top U.S. law school?

I came out of that conversation feeling bipolar. On the one hand, I was elated to find that this group of political conservatives was not a figment of my imagination. It existed. I was not alone. Students agreed with me about the politics of the law school, the lack of discourse, and the most explosive issue of all, affirmative action. On the other hand, those same students felt silenced. Even knowing I was speaking out, this group would not discuss their views on our campus.

I am distraught by this situation. In a country that prides itself on freedom of opinion and public debate, and more specifically on a campus that is known for its political outspokenness, a group of students with strong views sits silent. When we finally make our way to each other, we speak freely, but all the while we watch for who is passing in the hall. This underground society exists, but it should not be a secret. We are not alone, but we cannot know that if we are silenced by fear. We need to come out into the open and speak. Yes, on campus.

The 1964 Civil Rights Act provides that "All persons shall be entitled to be free . . . from discrimination or segregation of any kind on the ground of race . . . if such segregation is . . . required by any . . . order of a State." When did "all persons" cease to include whites? Proposition 209, which of course is now in full force as Article 1 §31 of the Constitution of the State of California, states: "The state shall not discriminate against, or give preferential treatment to, any individual on the basis of race . . . ." Affirmative action applies these words to blacks, Asians, Indians, Eskimos, and purple people from Mars, but not to whites.

Affirmative action is a tense issue, and emotions run high. Here at Boalt I have found an incredible lack of diversity, but I do not mean in skin color. I refer to viewpoints.

I voted for Proposition 209 and I strongly oppose affirmative action. You can call me a racist if you wish, but you would be wrong. The majority of California voters agree with me. However, listening to other students at Boalt I wonder how many of you do. I know I am not the only one.

Affirmative action is legally sanctioned discrimination. Under its policies, perfectly capable people with potential to succeed are told that they cannot have the opportunity because of their skin color or gender. Sounds like something out of the nineteenth century. Barbaric, perhaps.

A lot of justifications are presented for affirmative action. Among them are that it repays "minorities" for past discrimination, puts everyone on equal footing, increases diversity (however defined), gives those who would otherwise not have a chance the opportunity to succeed, makes up for bad childhood, and advances the races. ("Minorities" is in quotation marks because the numbers do not justify the term in a growing number of situations, including in my school district, where whites are a numerical minority.) In reality, affirmative action discriminates against whites and allows

---

[1] This article first appeared in Boalt Hall's *Cross-Examiner*, a student publication.

substandard professionals to enter the marketplace.

I first take issue with the idea of repayment for past discrimination. Why should I repay anyone for the past? Granted, people suffered a great deal, but I did not do anything. Neither did my ancestors. Most of us being directly affected by affirmative action programs have suffered no detriment ourselves, nor committed any wrong. I heard a Boalt professor say that the Constitution is not color-blind, and that we should discriminate against whites for just as long as we discriminated against nonwhites, meaning one hundred and some years. The Constitution is only as color-blind as we make it. If we insist on seeing color, it will, too. Also, two wrongs do not make a right. If it was wrong to discriminate against other races, why is it okay to discriminate against whites?

Second, affirmative action supposedly puts everyone on equal footing. No it does not. It puts white people, especially males, a step below everyone else. Giving preference to one class of people over another is inherently unequal.

I find the third justification comical: affirmative action increases diversity. It does increase the rainbow of skin colors. That is not diversity in any meaningful sense. To define diversity as such is only to perpetuate pigeonholing based upon race. To me, diversity is a range of viewpoints and experiences. In this respect Berkeley is incredibly homogenous. The conservative view is practically unrepresented. I prefer to be surrounded by whites with varied backgrounds and opinions than people of several races who were all raised in homes similar to mine and have similar views. This can easily happen under affirmative action.

It happens when the program states that Asians, for example, get preference in admissions. Many of my high school classmates will be admitted before I will. Those who receive preferential treatment outnumber whites in my district. They will not bring significantly different experiences to the classroom. These are kids who grew up across the street from me, attended the same schools, and, if anything, had more parental encouragement than I did.

How do you justify telling a kid who has done well and is prepared for college that he cannot go because a kid of another race who did not do as well gets to go in his place? There is no justification.

Affirmative action is supposed to help the people who would otherwise not have a chance. Why would they not have a chance? Is it because they are victims of this or that, often stated as the oppressive white world? Or is it because they leaned on those crutches so long that they never really tried? Let us all stop being victims. Take control of our own destinies and responsibility for our own fates. Do not ask for special treatment.

Asking for special treatment does two things. First, it tells the world that you are not capable of making it on your own. Is that the message anyone wants to send? People will not advance and better themselves if they tell the world they cannot do it themselves. Second, it signals that you think other people's work and abilities are undeserving of recognition. Do not expect respect from those people. The world owes each of us nothing.

A fifth justification for affirmative action is that it makes up for bad childhoods, to paraphrase the argument. Not all parents encourage their children. Not everyone has a good home environment. These experiences are not confined to nonwhites. All kinds of people have lousy parents. A bad childhood is a bad excuse. We are not victims of our upbringing unless we allow ourselves to be. If we allow ourselves to be, we deserve no breaks.

One of the most hypocritical arguments is that affirmative action helps advance the races. It helps us in our struggle for a color-blind society. How can we "become" color-blind all the while highlighting our differences with fireworks? We end up pitted against each other based on race instead of forgetting that we look different. To advance we must advance ourselves. Each of us must stop complaining about the past and look to the future.

Affirmative action allows people of lesser, and sometimes inadequate, skills to become doctors and lawyers while freezing out those of greater talent. There was a study done recently on doctors admitted to medical school under affirmative action policies. It said that eventually their careers were similar to those of doctors admitted without the policies. Personally, I do not want to be one of the patients waiting for "eventually" to happen. The study does not mention Dr. Patrick Chavis, though. He is the "minority" man who was admitted to medical school, despite his lower test scores, ahead of the infamous white Mr. Bakke. Dr. Chavis, hailed by Senator Ted Kennedy as "a perfect example" of racial preferences helping communities, recently had his license suspended by the California State Medical Board for his "inabilities to perform some of the most basic duties required of a physician." Apparently, one of his patients died unnecessarily, and two others nearly did. How many die-hard affirmative action supporters are making appointments with him?[2]

These supposed justifications set forth in support of affirmative action fall flat. Dr. Chavis is an example of why race should not be a factor considered in awarding anything at all.

We should be given jobs and admitted to schools based on our abilities. Do not tell me that my achievements are less valid because I am white. They do not have anything to do with my color. I am not saying that any Boalt student does not belong here because of his or her race. I am saying that if they belong here, it is not because of their race. It is because of their achievements and abilities.

The achievements and abilities that deem us deserving vary. One of us may be an especially talented advocate, while another may have exceptional reasoning and writing skills. It is not all about grades and test scores, but those things are evidence of our capabilities. Our skin color is evidence of nothing but our lineage.

Discrimination is imposing a disadvantage on a group of people. The 1964 Civil Rights Act, hailed as one of the greatest pieces of legislation in our nation's history, prohibits discrimination, as does the California Constitution. Giving an advantage to one class of people is necessarily imposing a disadvantage on another. That is affirmative action, and it is discrimination.

---

[2] See *Wall Street Journal*, August 27, 1997, A12 and *Los Angeles Times*, August 26, 1997, A21.

Behind the Tattered Curtain of Racial Preferences

By Brian D. Wyatt

After matriculating as a first-year student at Boalt Hall, I found myself focused on two overarching thoughts. The first was, wow, everyone here sure is intelligent. The second was, wow, my colleagues may be preternaturally gifted, but, as far as politics are concerned, they seem to be on the same monolithic page. It wasn't until months later that I discovered there were more than two Republicans on campus. This was amazingly ironic, because from the first session of orientation, Boalt had been offering itself kudos for being a "diverse" institution. At the same time there was no Republican group to offer an alternative to the entrenched Boalt Democrats. The underlying current of any "debate" appeared to center on one topic: how can we be the best liberals we can be?

Perhaps nowhere has this quest for liberal nirvana been more noticeable than in the absence of desire for diverse opinion regarding racial preferences. The only noteworthy "discussion" of the matter has been a series of immature demonstrations that have included the interrupting of class to ask white students to surrender their seats to minority visitors, the spraying of graffiti, the heckling of anti-preferences speakers at the one "debate" held on the matter, and the rumored pummeling of a Caucasian piñata in the quad. Feelings have been intense. Diversity of expression has been minimal.

We white, middle-class males know what it's like to face institutionalized discrimination on the basis of our skin color. In and out of Boalt Hall, Caucasian reaction to this has been mixed. Some have said, "Well, we deserve it," because of the reprehensible racial record of America or because of the indifference shown by many Caucasians to the historical plight of minorities. Others have said we ought to endure this injustice due to so much contemporary discrimination. Some have just gotten mad, cynical, or indifferent. Most have simply pressed on with their lives in silent resignation. The voters of California, on the other hand, decided it best to scrap the whole scheme when they approved Proposition 209.

My purpose in writing is not to repeat the litany of critiques of racial preferences in legal education, or in life. Much has been said about how preferences and quotas are unfair to those who have by hard effort earned positions they cannot assume because of their fair skin. Plenty has also been propounded about how "affirmative action," as it is benignly called, actually stigmatizes minorities, rather than ultimately advancing them.

Instead, I wish to point out a social criticism that many times has been overlooked. I begin with some awful statistics. In testimony before the State Senate Select Committees on Higher Education Admissions and Outreach, UCLA law school Dean Susan Westerberg Prager noted that only 103 African Americans and 224 Hispanics who sat for the test in 1996 had a Law School Admissions Test (LSAT) score of 160 or more and an undergraduate grade average of 3.25 or better. In stark contrast, 7,715 Caucasians scored at least that high. To get into a top tier law school, like Boalt Hall, a college graduate must usually score at or above 164 on the LSAT and have a minimum GPA of 3.5. While there were 2,460 whites in that range, the number of qualifying blacks and Hispanics were limited to 16 and 45, respectively.[1]

Considering that the LSAT has proven to be an excellent proxy for success in law school and in legal practice, these numbers are

---

[1] Michael Ueda, "Affirmative Action Focuses Scrutiny on Legal Education," *California Law Student Journal*, April 1998, 6.

alarmingly dismal. According to Michael Ueda of the Daily Journal Corporation, the 1996 State Bar records show that, "After graduation from the three [California] state schools – Boalt Hall, UCLA and University of California, Davis – Hispanics and blacks passed the bar at rates 20 percentage points lower than Caucasians, but are still well above state averages."[2]

What these numbers do not prove is that underrepresented minority groups are inherently incapable of competing with others. What they do indicate is that decades of affirmative action have not resulted in much more than a cover-up of a serious problem in our society. Racial preferences have been a sham.

Affirmative action in education was an idea intended to relieve a nasty symptom of social failure, namely the absence of a real minority presence in the more "noble" occupations in society. The source of this problem, however, has always begun way before college or law school – it has been a crisis in our schools and in our homes. We have exchanged personal responsibility for fulfilling our narcissistic-hedonistic fantasies. Instead of concerning ourselves with the welfare of our fellow citizens, we do things like surrender 15 years of our lifetimes (on average) to television-watching. We have sloughed off the education of our kids (both morally and intellectually) to strangers, and have subsumed the importance of their emotional welfare to our selfish goals of pleasure, power, and wealth. The crisis we have is a spiritual one, and it doesn't go away when we only deal with it symbolically. This is the elephant in our living room.

Needing to justify our personal excesses and lack of concern for the plight of others, we have allowed decades of deception to emerge. Instead of addressing the root causes of discrimination against and under-performance by minorities, those who hold power positions in our culture have urged that it is our social duty to merely support institutionalized discrimination against those of non-minority categories. In so doing, we can make the statistics show the appropriate number of minorities fill our schools and our workplaces. These are

---

[2] Michael Ueda, "Bar Pass Rates Display Sharp Racial Disparity," *California Law Student Journal*, April 1998, 10.

the same people, like our President and Vice President, who send their kids to upper-crust private schools while urging urban youths to play midnight basketball. That's symbolic nonsense.

Fudging the numbers with affirmative action, at the expense of many competent, hard-working Americans, does not make the adult minority beneficiaries suddenly ready to participate coequally in society. I submit that liberals and conservatives alike have shown remarkable indifference to the ill-prepared minority communities. Many liberal supporters of affirmative action haven't needed to care sincerely because their program makes things "look OK." (For some crazy reason, most establishment liberals have convinced themselves and many in minority communities that as long as the numbers look good, our society is really fair or that all one can expect is a weak paper justice in America.) Many conservative critics of racial preferences seem only to want them to end so that their own social group will no longer face irrational discrimination.

So when a majority of California voters approved the demise of racial quotas in the government and education sectors, what happened next? Liberals got mad because the entitlement program that made everything look better was suddenly extinguished. Conservatives were overjoyed because now the state didn't officially sanction injustice. But what about the fact that so many minority students are still finding it so hard or lack the desire to compete on their own?

If we want to put an end to this injustice, I can see only one long-term solution. All of us – in every ethnic community – must take it upon ourselves to be responsible for our actions and to reach out to those who are situated differently. It may sound simplistic and silly, but it's about time for the children of white parents and of black parents to start voluntarily playing together in the same sandbox. We must intentionally cultivate interracial friendships. As I survey the whole of our society, there appears to be only one institution that is slowly, but surely, making a start in this direction: the Christian church.

When these issues are addressed as a spiritual problem (by groups such as the Promise Keepers and churches such as the First

Presbyterian Church of Berkeley), things start to change: racial groups are beginning to find reconciliation. There is hope for America, but it isn't in the empty panacea of reverse discrimination.

We ought to take an honest look at our society and see if this hope for our country has something more to do with the power of God working through people than the illusory power of the state. As long as we make our personal ambitions or social engineering via our government to be our deity, the spiritual crisis will continue. Those of us white males who have faced the injustice of institutionalized discrimination have a particular moral burden to conduct a search for this hope. After all, we, too, know what it's like to be without it.

CHAPTER EIGHT

THE DOUBLE STANDARD

The following two essays describe a
dangerous double standard. It is
imperative that law students not only
honor the faculty of reason and the
need to feed it diverse opinions, but
also respect the diverse backgrounds
of other students – including religion.

Raw Hypocrisy
By Jason Beutler

I admit that in coming to Boalt Hall I had some reservations. This law school is known for its radical leftist tendencies. However, through the storm of groups advocating far-from-mainstream causes shines what appears to be the silver lining in it all – tolerance of others' ideas and a diverse environment. Here, so the story goes, is a school where ideas can be discussed in an environment of tolerance and respect for people with a whole range of diverse ideas. But what exactly do tolerance and diversity mean at Boalt Hall? Given my experiences here during the recent months, I would say those words at Boalt Hall are often used to advocate what amounts to the antithesis of true tolerance and diversity.

A seemingly uncontroversial definition of tolerance would seem to be avoiding name-calling and wild, unsubstantiated claims about groups we disagree with. Certainly, this is not a radical definition of the word. Yet, this definition is constantly violated here, which tells me the rhetoric about tolerance and diversity must go to a quite different definition.

The most personal exposure I had with this double standard for tolerance came in criminal law class last semester. One day we were discussing whether ordinary negligence was a high enough standard to use in convicting an American Indian couple that failed to secure medical treatment for their baby, who had a severely infected tooth that eventually led to the child's death. One student who showed an apparently strong interest in defending "diverse, underprivileged" groups piped up and said: "Well, those parents had a right to be concerned about taking their child to get medical help. Those Mormons were trying to commit cultural genocide on the Indians, taking away their children if they tried to get state help." As a devout member of the Church of Jesus Christ of Latter-Day Saints (Mormons is a short nickname) I found the comments highly offensive and untrue. My first reaction was to raise my hand and tell the woman exactly how wrong she was. But then I thought "what does this personal assault have to do with the class? Why dignify her remarks by even making a reply?" So I let it go, and so did everybody else in the class.

Her attack on Mormons as baby snatchers committing cultural genocide went by without response. Even writing this is almost more of a reply than I want to make to that remark, but I bring it up because it symbolizes a whole range of insensitive, intolerant remarks I hear at Boalt Hall with some regularity. Similarly, comments have been made throughout my time here about people who "cling to traditional family values" and religious affiliation. They are typically met by the same passive acceptance. I guess at Boalt Hall it is acceptable to take shots at minority groups if conservatives are among them.

In contrast, over the course of my classes, students have made somewhat insensitive remarks about homosexuals or preferences given to minority businesses. These comments have always led several students who promote diverse lifestyle choice to comment on how "bigoted" and ugly these remarks are. Teachers have also reminded the students of the need for tolerance in their dialogue with each other. Why is it that tolerance is an issue only when certain groups are targeted? Why are comments only bigoted when they are insensitive to homosexuals and affirmative action programs for minorities and not when they demean people who hold strong religious beliefs or support traditional family values?

Tolerance as used by the Left seems really to mean respecting and accepting the extreme Left's moral values and policy goals. According to such logic, there is no reason to classify calling groups on the Right names as intolerant. Thus, the Left's definition of tolerance seems to be the exact opposite of tolerance as traditionally understood. To say that name-calling should only be permitted in one direction seems both intolerant and unfair. Diversity has a similarly antithetical meaning at Boalt Hall. Diversity here means people from groups that agree with leftist values. An example of this is the way that religious groups are classed as a monolithic group of deluded individuals. In reality, different religious groups bring diverse belief structures to the discussion of legal issues and make for a fuller academic debate, but they do not fit into the diversity paradigm at Boalt because they typically embrace family values and not the any-lifestyle-you-chose-is-as-good-as-any-other (as long as it is not traditional) agenda of the Left. I think tolerance and diversity as traditionally defined are important things for worthwhile academic discussion, which is why I have a hard time supporting the Berkeley version of them.

Please, Remain Silent
By Naomi Harlin

Overall, I have had a good experience at Boalt, despite my unpopular political beliefs and moral convictions. I have particularly enjoyed seminars in which students have the opportunity to share their understanding of the law and the reasons behind this understanding. It is impressive to be in a group discussion of intelligent and rational peers.

Imagine a room set up for a group discussion. Around a long rectangular table stand chairs. You can only sit on the left side of the table if you have liberal thoughts. People who advocate individual freedom (like abortion, or gay rights), or advocate governmental intervention for the "under-represented" (like affirmative action) choose to sit at this side of the table. The other side of the rectangle, the right side, has seats for those who are conservative. You can only sit on this side of the table if you advocate a limited government.

What is important is that each side of the table agrees to enter into rational dialogue with each other. Each side recognizes that things are relative, and no matter how strongly one feels about an issue the other side has a right to their beliefs. At the head of the table sits the "neutral" discussion leader (if one can ever be "neutral" is a discussion for a later topic).

Of course, such a sitting is very simplistic, for there are extreme radicals who will sit at either side of table, as well as people who could identify with both the liberal and conservative ideas. Indeed, given any different issue, I might find myself sitting on either side of the table. I thought about writing about the radicals who have torn down The Federalist Society's flyers, or who wrote "Satanus Rex" on the Christians at Boalt's bulletin board. But, of course, there are radicals, on the Left and on the Right. It is easy to slam either side by pointing to the actions of these radicals. Besides, for the most part, I have encountered people at Boalt who disagree with me, but are reasonable about it. So, back to the group discussion table.

To me, the room where the table is located represents the atmosphere of Boalt. Of course, the left side of the table has many more people sitting at it than the right side. Because of this unbalance, the right side often doesn't get heard over the multitude of loud voices from the left side. In fact, those sitting on the Right even get intimidated by the multitudes on the Left so that they often don't speak up, even when they get the chance, for fear of causing more noise. This phenomenon, however, is nothing special to Boalt. It just so happens that a majority of the students identify with liberal beliefs. But, I honestly believe that if this same table was set up, for example, at Chicago Law, that the Right's voice might be louder, and then the Left might feel intimidated to speak up.

Given my political stance, it seems obvious that I would take a seat at the right of the table. And, on many issues, this would be the appropriate place for me. But, actually I sit at the end of the table. Chairs at the end are reserved for people whose beliefs are not considered reasonable, but who are allowed to enter the discussion anyway because relativity demands that all people have a right to believe what they want. All views, even mine, have to be tolerated. However, toleration doesn't mean that the views are given any legitimacy.

I sit at the end of the table because I am a Christian. Being a Christian is not something to do only on Sundays, or in the privacy of my own home, but is at the heart of who I am. But, at one point during a debate, a friend asked me why I was a Christian. My friend thought it was strange that someone who was educated enough to be at Boalt could also reasonably believe in God and His Son, Jesus. Such beliefs, my friend believed, were for the common populace, but not for an academic setting.

I have been in debates about the hottest of topics – affirmative action, abortion, gay rights, the death penalty. I am allowed to believe whatever I want, but in private. I'm asked not to bring my religion to the public square, even though it is the basis of my identity. So, I often sit at the end of the table, not invited by either the liberals or conservatives to enter the discussion.

CHAPTER NINE

ATTEMPTS AT GOOD HUMOR

One natural response to difficult or oppressive circumstances, even threats to free speech and intellectual freedom, is humor, or at least an attempt to see the comedy in the middle of what feels like tragedy. Sometimes, as in Eastern Block countries before the fall of communism, the humor can be wry, bitter, and sweetly hopeful at the same time. When outsiders look in at a situation fraught with problems, the distance they bring can produce a kind of humor that reveals as it shocks. Insiders, in contrast, are so aware of their shock effect that they expect less laughter than scorn, and hence see a reason to write anonymously.

Almost Nonfiction*

Anonymous

September 30, 1997

"Hi, my name is Rebecca, and I'm white."
"Hi, my name is Alan, and I'm white."

One by one, they stood up, introduced themselves, and sat down. Why did I start White Persons Anonymous? Because it's the only place at Boalt where I don't feel I have to apologize for the color of my skin. And I can express my views without fear that I will be called a racist, a Nazi, or a member of the KKK.

I didn't think about skin color much growing up. Mostly I was focused on getting by. In my hometown of Tutwiler, Mississippi, there wasn't a whole lot of talk about race. Tutwiler is in the Mississippi River delta area, and it's one of many small, destitute little towns in what is the poorest state in our nation. Race wasn't really much of an issue. Black or white, we were all poor.

I started working in the cotton fields illegally at age 11 to help support my family. Large corporations own most of the land in this

---

* Editors' Note: This piece was submitted anonymously along with a note stating that it is fictitious.

area. So, despite the fact that the land around the Mississippi River delta is fertile and productive, most people don't benefit from the riches generated by the land. They just work as sharecroppers, doing harvesting, planting, or whatever they can to make ends meet.

I was the first person from my family to graduate from high school. I got a scholarship to college. Then, I came here to Boalt. On our first day of class, there was a demonstration and a press conference with numerous speakers denigrating our class and what we stood for. I'd never much been into politics. I voted Republican because my father and uncle said it was the better party. My reason for going to law school was that I wanted to get involved in local government. I'd like to try and bring some industry to my hometown, and also work on improving Mississippi's very inadequate primary education system.

I really don't see why I should have to apologize for being here. I've been through a lot to get here, and I'm sure all of my classmates have as well. We're all qualified. Why can't we all just judge each other by who we are, not by what we look like?

October 10, 1997

I've been kidnapped! The left-wing radicals planted a mole in our group, determined that I was the leader, and have decided to "deprogram" me. They have tied me to a chair and forced me to watch "Berkeley in the Sixties" over and over again. They have confiscated my car, my watch, and my money. I am resolved to stand firm in my beliefs.

October 15, 1997

I am beginning to have doubts about my previous rigid position. Perhaps "diversity" really is more important than equal rights. After all, white people have gotten a lot of breaks over the years.

November 1, 1997

Now I understand how truly undeserving I am. I have led a life of privilege as a white person. I am taking a spot at Boalt that should rightfully have gone to someone else. Someone who, despite not getting admitted on his/her merits, can contribute a lot more to diversity and academic excellence than I can.

November 30, 1997

We had a great day today – in fact the past week has been terrific. We had a demonstration and we've started pulling fire alarms. Yesterday we took a break from the revolution so we could interview for firm jobs. Then back to the struggle for equality! We're planning to try and get arrested because we think that will have a profound effect on the position of the Regents of the University of California.

December 15, 1997

In my more lucid moments, I remember a time when I had different beliefs. A time when I wanted people at law school to judge me on my merits, not on my skin color. But then I take another hit from the bong, and everything is OK again.

Constipation of the Brainium

By Grant Peters, M.D.

There was a pleasant drizzle from the overcast sky when the call came in. Bad internal distress at Boalt Hall, could I make a house call? I was awful busy. The office was full of decapitated HMO patients wanting to be seen for referrals to the real doctors (specialists), but this sounded interesting. I called my buddy, a gastroenterologist at the big medical school across the bay. He said he'd meet me in Café Zeb (the law school café) at 11:00 a.m. I left a referral pad with my nurse practitioner but told her the cost of the referrals would come out of her 401K contribution. I sneaked out the back door. It was dangerous but I had to go. After all, the lawyer wannabes would probably sue me if I didn't. My buddy thought it sounded like a disorder of idea digestion. Possibly constipation of the brainium. Interesting clinical question, he said.

Another thing. Did lawyers think or was it all reflex? I'd heard from friends that lawyers did really think, at least sometimes, but usually not for too long. Mostly they just picked out an idea that sounded good (or had a big retainer) and argued about it. Normal people think about their ideas and question them. Sometimes they even change their minds. But lawyers are rumored to be different. No right, no wrong, just argue. "Legalesque mentation" they called it in medical school. Dangerous and often contagious with sufficient exposure.

After coffee at Zeb's we ventured to walk the halls. We even snuck into a couple of classes of the wannabes pretending to be seniors trying to decide between Boalt and UCLA. (We were going to say Stanford but remembered we had families.) We talked to some of the students in the hall between class. Even got invited to a bar review, but we didn't feel like actually studying law. We just wanted to check on the wannabes. Finally we'd had enough and retreated to Zeb's to write up the consultation report.

Most of the wannabes are still thinking. The healthy ones can question their ideas and actually wonder if they might be wrong some of the time. They can eliminate ideas OK so they have room for new ones. They still are aware a coin has two sides. Some of the wannabes, though, are real sick. My buddy called it mental constipation. An idea gets in and won't leave. After a while there is not much room for new ideas. Coins stop having two sides. The world become a bad photocopy where all the shades of grey are gone. Black and white, that's it, and they fixate on one or the other. The pressure in the brainium builds up and makes hearing hard. So they talk more, but it's always the same. Always they think they are right. It is really hard for them to listen because there is no more room inside for new ideas. When questioned, they sometimes yell and shout from the pressure of the cherished idea trying to keep out anything that might challenge it. No room. No room. Anal retentive in the head. Out of disk space. The processor is shut off already. They already act like lawyers even though some just started. A pity. And no known treatment. It was sad.

We found the correct CPT codes (so we could bill) and wrote the report. My buddy said the healthy ones should do fine as long as they stayed humble and honest. Those that were humble enough to doubt themselves and honest enough to admit it would be okay. They would listen and make room for new ideas. They might even talk sometimes if the sick ones weren't around to fuss and call them Republicans. They could become some of the rare thinking attorneys we had heard about (most of them do malpractice defense). But those whose heads were already so full they could not listen were doomed.

I was back in the office by 3:00 p.m. It was still full of the decapitated HMO patients. The nurse practitioner had done well. She had only given out two referral slips. One to a patient whose broken leg had not yet healed after four months of ACE™ wraps and aspirin, and the other to a gentleman with a minor skin rash whose daughter happened to be a lawyer. Only 85 patients left to see in 2 hours. It was good to be back.

CHAPTER TEN

THE END OF THE INDIVIDUAL?

Could it be that the habit of thinking in the increasingly popular terms of identity politics and political correctness is bringing about the end of the individual in America? The preceding essays suggest that at the very least there has been an erosion of the concept of the individual and the practice of individual liberty. As James Madison wrote in The Federalist Papers: "I believe there are more instances of the abridgment of the freedom of the people by gradual and silent encroachments of those in power than by violent and sudden usurpations." As this last essay suggests, whether abridgment will be permitted and usurpations brooked is a crucial question. To go forth anonymously is to give in, and yet, to render oneself truly anonymous, if only for the sake of argument, is perhaps to serve a wake-up call to anyone who seeks to remain an individual.

Truly Anonymous

Anonymous

In the true spirit of Boalt Hall, this essay will be published anonymously. My name does not matter, nor do my personal achievements. My grades, test scores, and leadership positions are all just a product of my affluent upbringing – they, too, are irrelevant. There is only one thing that matters here at Boalt. Hence, there is only one thing that I will reveal about myself. I AM WHITE.

I learned this lesson in a criminal law class during my first semester at this "liberal" law school. The class was taught by a famous criminal law professor who was visiting Boalt for the semester. After just a few classes, he had earned the respect of many members of his class for being a sensitive and sincere communicator of legal knowledge. His name, Joshua Dressler, deserves to be mentioned. The reading for the day covered, among other things, the self-defense case involving Bernhard Goetz, who became famous by defending himself against four screwdriver-wielding youths in a New York City subway.

Halfway through the class, without notice, two doors on both sides of the professor swung open, and into the classroom flooded a mass of unfamiliar faces. Many of the faces did not belong at Boalt – they had not been accepted. Most of these faces were black. A few were Latino. Immediately, a student in the class stood up from her chair, abruptly interrupting the professor's lecture, and began rattling off some diatribe about the importance of diversity and other empty slogans. In an angry tone, she then placed a request – that white students of the Class of 2000, who had been admitted to Boalt purely due to their achievement and merit, give up their seats for "minority" students who had not gained admission to the Class of 2000. Several students surrendered their chairs to students whose sole justification for being in the class was the color of their skin.

I froze in my chair. I could not move. I could not understand. Tears welled up in my eyes. To these people, "race" was all that mattered. Everything else was meaningless. My body began to shake, as if I was in the process of being gutted from the inside out, leaving only a thin layer of skin to show for myself and my existence.

After addressing the demonstration as inappropriate, the professor tried to continue his lecture. He informed the class that he had a duty to teach only those students enrolled in the class (who had "earned" the privilege to study at Boalt), and would not incorporate the intruders into the class discussion. Many of these "new" faces sneered at the professor. The professor, who is white, earnestly tried to continue his lecture on self-defense.

The class ended early when a student, one of the few outspoken conservatives, mockingly asked the professor: Given that this doctrine of self-defense is so complicated, why not just have a numerical quota on the number of people each year who should be sent to prison and released from prison, rather than having to face the difficulty of a person-to-person test of who merits to go to prison and who does not?

The professor responded by dismissing the class. He could not or did not want to go on.

At Boalt, one of the most highly regarded law schools in the nation, I have witnessed the death of the individual. I was asked to apologize for my ability. I was asked to apologize for my success. Those people who considered themselves "victims" saw me as a parasite simply because I am white. They believe that it is morally correct for my interests to be sacrificed in any manner they please for whatever they hold to be in the "public good." I have never held a slave. My family did not arrive in America until well after the Civil War. If I am guilty, then no such innocence exists. In their eyes, I am anonymous but for my race. I sign this piece accordingly, as a white male, disgusted by the climate here at Boalt and terrified where the future will take us.

PART THREE: The Future

If there is any principle of the
Constitution that more imperatively
calls for attachment than any other
it is the principle of free thought –
not free thought for those who agree
with us but freedom for the
thought we hate.

OLIVER WENDELL HOLMES

If there be time to expose through
discussion the falsehood and fallacies,
to avert the evil by the process of
education, the remedy to be applied
is more speech, not enforced silence.

LOUIS D. BRANDEIS

The Future
By David Wienir and Marc Berley

Somewhere along the road from the 1960's to the 1990's, the hard-won right of free speech has been trampled on. Back in 1963, President John F. Kennedy declared: "If we cannot end now our differences, at least we can help make the world safe for diversity."[1] So far, the Boalt Hall community has failed to make itself safe for the differences of which true diversity is composed.

For better or worse, students and academics are the intellectual bodyguards of truth. Law schools especially play an essential role in shaping American culture and values. A law school such as Boalt Hall trains America's future lawyers, judges, and legislators.

It can be safely asserted that an informed society must be a free society, and a free society must be informed. A free society depends on the honesty and integrity of its academic institutions. It is well known that whoever controls the past controls the future. How students are taught in law school will have a profound effect on the way society defines equality, justice, freedom, liberty, and other essential principles of our legal system and society.

The Language War
Many students and faculty at America's law schools have been staging a radical assault on the English language. Words once neutral

---

[1] John F. Kennedy, Address at American University, June 10, 1963.

have been inconspicuously redefined and distorted into centerpieces of a destabilizing agenda, allowing a politically radical minority to command the moral high ground, and making it nearly impossible for any reasonable, good-hearted person to disagree. Through this distortion of language, they have created an environment in which dissent is itself often seen as morally evil.

Saying that one is for diversity, public interest, and equal opportunity is one thing. Defining the terms is another. At Berkeley, "diversity" is ubiquitously defined in racial terms: race matters – ideas do not. This monolithic definition purports disingenuously to speak for all minorities. Similarly, the "public interest" is defined to include only the members of the public who share an agenda that includes opposition to Proposition 209. "Equal opportunity" requires blameless white men, as well as certain "over-represented" minorities, to be sacrificed at the altar of racial justice in the name of "diversity" and "public interest." In other words, rather than seek equality of opportunity, people plead for and machinate to achieve equality of results. Few will ever confess to their forcible linguistic distortions, for confession would render their power obsolete.

Language has come to be used as both a control mechanism and a weapon. By dressing up their radical agenda in altruist terminology, the 'diversity' protesters at Berkeley have shielded themselves from much criticism. Fearing reprisal, few dare question, or even define, their motives. Through this monopoly, the 'diversity' protesters attempt to destroy their enemies – publicly denouncing anyone who disagrees with their agenda, usually by calling them ugly names that mainly stick.

The most tragic consequence of the distortions of language is that Boalt – like American universities in general – has come to seem like a modern-day Tower of Babel. To the detriment of civil debate, individual words have come to have different meanings for different groups.

The real problem, however, is even more disturbing. What could be worse than having separate communities speaking cacophonous languages with incompatible meanings? Many appear to want to establish a Tower of Babel – a self-deconstructing, anti-rational

Postmodern America that lays the groundwork for seemingly opportunistic balkanization. In the absence of clear meanings for words once largely understood by all, demagogues can make a linguistic grab for political power. In such a context, new arbiters of the political lexicon may step in and define all the terms in ways that suit their special political interests. Indeed, this has been a motivating principle of the radical revolution in the academic world in the last thirty years. Those who wish to change reality, or at least the way people may perceive and confront reality, understand the power of definition, and of controlling it.

Writing about the revolution in Corcyra in *The Peloponnesian War*, the Greek historian Thucydides teaches an ancient lesson about the power of re-definition:

> So revolutions broke out in city after city, and in places where the revolutions occurred late the knowledge of what had happened previously in other places caused still new extravagances of revolutionary zeal, expressed by an elaboration in the methods of seizing power and by unheard of atrocities in revenge. To fit in with the change of events, words, too, had to change their usual meanings. What used to be described as a thoughtless act of aggression was now regarded as the courage one would expect to find in a party member....[2]

What Thucydides saw as the awful consequences of revolution has much in common with the practices of people who have demonstrated "extravagances of revolutionary zeal" at Boalt Hall: "ability to understand a question from all sides meant that one was totally unfitted for action." Indeed, "anyone who held violent opinions could always be trusted, and anyone who objected to them became a suspect."[3]

---

[2] Thucydides, *The Peloponnesian War*, trans. Rex Warner (New York: Penguin, 1954) 242.

[3] *The Peloponnesian War*, 242.

Once words and principles were radically redefined, Thucydides explains, civil society began to fall completely apart: "Family relations were a weaker tie than party membership....Revenge was more important than self-preservation....Love of power, operating through greed and through personal ambition, was the cause of all these evils." As Thucydides writes, "in professing to serve the public interest [party leaders] were seeking to win the prizes for themselves. In their struggles for ascendancy nothing was barred; terrible indeed were the actions to which they committed themselves, and in taking revenge they went farther still. Here they were deterred neither by the claims of justice nor by the interest of the state...."[4]

Diversity, public interest, equal opportunity. How the meanings of these words have been distorted at UC Berkeley – and elsewhere! Diversity has come to mean homogeneity. Public interest has come to mean self-interest. Equal opportunity has come to mean a perverse egalitarianism.

Without a common definition of the crucial words in any society, meaningful discussion cannot occur. Where differences exist, meaningful discourse can only occur in an atmosphere of tolerance, of willingness to define terms mutually and debate civilly.

For this reason, traditional liberal arts education in the Western intellectual tradition can provide needed common ground. Unfortunately, the movement against free speech for all at Boalt Hall is part of a larger movement that seeks to rid college and university classrooms of the Western intellectual tradition – indeed, of authors such as Thucydides himself. The war against Western civilization – Plato, Aristotle, Locke, Jefferson, etc. – has been waged. In some places, such as American universities, it has been too close to won. "Hey, hey, ho, ho, Western Civ. has got to go," students chanted not many years ago at Stanford University, an institution of higher learning that jettisoned a core curriculum in the Western tradition as if it were excess cultural baggage.

The damage done to American society by depriving students of common ground upon which to disagree civilly, already sadly evi-

---

4   *The Peloponnesian War*, 243-44.

dent, is likely to become unimaginable. As Mortimer J. Adler once explained, "Argument is unprofitable – worse than that, unintelligible – when opponents do not share some common ground....Between the man who obeys the rule not to contradict himself and the man who finds nothing repugnant in answering Yes and No to the same question, there can be no argument. There is an issue between them, but the position each takes reduces the other to silence."[5]

The Narrowing of Discourse

The Boalt community, as part of a larger academic and social movement, has fostered the transformation of matters of opinion into matters of fact, and of matters of fact into matters of opinion. In doing so, it has severely hampered the possibility for true diversity on campus. A politically powerful homogeneous minority now gets to establish the facts, sanction opinions, meet out rewards and punishments, and determine who shall have the right to speak freely.

During the 1960's, student protesters dedicated themselves to the kind of free speech that the great liberal John Stuart Mill did so much to define and defend. Today at Berkeley, in contrast, those who claim to define free speech are the last ones to defend it. Mill would not like the Berkeley campus of today:

> Strange that they should imagine that they are not assuming infallibility, when they acknowledge that there should be free discussion on all subjects which can possibly be *doubtful*, but think that some particular principle or doctrine should be forbidden to be questioned because it is so *certain*, that is, because *they* are *certain* that it is certain. To call any proposition certain, while there is any one who would deny its certainty if permitted, but who is not permitted, is to assume that we ourselves, and those who agree with us, are the judges of certainty, and judges without hearing the other side.[6]

---

[5] Mortimer J. Adler, *The Great Ideas: A Syntopicon of Great Books of the Western World*, Vol. II (Chicago: Encyclopedia Britannica, Inc., 1952) 588.

[6] *On Liberty*, 22.

At Boalt Hall, and at other schools nationwide, education is being compromised by a loss of intellectual freedom that is part of a larger attack on the power of reason. Intellectual freedom must be the paramount concern at any academic institution. It must not be compromised for the sake of radical social and ethnic interests.

Politically radical students appear to have seized control of Boalt Hall's mission. They occupy and lead the student council. They moderate the big debates. They sit on the admissions committee. They are partly responsible for hiring new faculty. They serve as academic tutors. In establishing the "new" agenda from the inside, they have sought to exclude or push out anyone who dares to disagree. These methods constitute rule by force, not persuasion by reason. What happens when a law school ceases to defend its faith in reason? Force replaces fairness; interest replaces justice. Unfortunately, Boalt Hall provides terrifying examples of how wrong things have gone in the world of higher education in America.

Recommendations

No brilliant strategy is needed to begin to remedy the aforementioned problem. No additional funds are required. No new faculty need be hired. Only two simple steps are necessary. First, everyone must acknowledge that the problem exists. Second, there needs to be honest re-commitment by all administrators, faculty, and students to the chief requirement of liberal education: respectful, civil, and open debate. Students should be encouraged to express their opinions as well as to listen to and digest opposing ideas. This will lead to institutions of greater civility, depth, and intellectual diversity – for everyone.

But there is, of course, a larger problem. The solution requires a far more complicated set of actions than a sanguine inducement to civil discourse could possibly effect. One cannot simply expect people to move in the direction of civility at the very same time law schools are themselves empowering an attack on reason – indeed, on the legitimacy of law itself. When a burgeoning law school discipline such as critical race theory says that the people of California have no moral right to vote on Proposition 209, and when prominent law professors such as Derrick Bell of Harvard assert that people should not dignify any criticism of critical race theory by responding to it, the very attack upon civil discourse makes the goal of civility elusive, to say the least.

We would like to be able to say that all people need to do is be more civil with each other, but civility requires willingness from two – indeed, many – sides. Unfortunately, this willingness is increasingly absent on college campuses today, and its absence is related to the trend of rejecting the traditional study of law and refusing to argue, if only for the sake of education, on two sides of every issue.

When the rule of law (even if it is an unpopular law such as Proposition 209) is branded an illegitimate form of societal oppression, when reason itself is counted as an illegitimate tool of oppression, there is little reason to expect that civility will increase rather than decrease. When antinomian group-think can appear to run a law school, as it did in 1997-98 at Boalt Hall, and when monolithic intolerance perpetrated by a few can bully a law school dean, it is time to understand that a concerted attack on civility has made its mark upon the top law schools in America.

Our greatest collective hope for civility and tolerance – indeed, for a better, if not harmonious, America – is the reassertion of basic liberal principles: respect for justice based in fairness; pursuit of truth rooted in reason; the right of free speech; and respect for all individuals and their individual rights. Nowhere is this more important than in our schools.

If those who recognize the problems can agree to take stock and act boldly now, perhaps we can save and nurture what is best in all of us. Hope can prevail, along with differences. New generations of American students can learn to disagree civilly. And as they ascend to positions of power in this country, they would be in a better position to address difficult problems and arrive at workable solutions.

Afterword

If I may be personal in this afterword, one of the saddest disappointments of my life has been watching one of the world's greatest creations, the American university, decline.

It has taken me a lifetime to stop venerating such words as "university" and "professor" and not to get goose bumps when I visit an esteemed college campus. When I was a senior in high school and received various college catalogues, I remember fingering those thick wonders believing they possessed wisdom.

Some people deem it an inevitable part of growing up to lose one's enthusiasms and become cynical. I do not. Many things, institutions included, excite me, now at fifty, as much as or even more than earlier in my life. For example, my awe at the achievement of the Founding Fathers actually grows with each year.

But I have, based on copious evidence, come to regard the American university – with individual noble exceptions and with the exception of departments of mathematics and the natural sciences – as the most intellectually closed, morally regressive, and socially intolerant of America's mainstream institutions. *The Diversity Hoax* documents with painful honesty and heart-wrenching detail numerous causes for profound disappointment at one prestigious university. And countless examples from other universities, sadly, abound.

Just how bad is the decay in the world of American higher education? When I read about a takeover of a university building, of a violent student disruption of the process of learning, or of a shouting-down of a speaker with whom the shouting students disagree, I must assume that the perpetrators are all radical ideologues from the Left. Even worse, I must assume also that the administration will do nothing to educate or discipline the young totalitarians, and that it may even support them – as regularly happens when students burn or steal copies of a university conservative newspaper. Why must I assume these things? Because no other assumptions would comport with present-day reality.

My assumptions are based on a few facts about American colleges and universities in their current state. Instead of facilitating the pursuit of truth, many American university professors (again, outside mathematics and the natural sciences) actually deny that truth exists or can ever be known.

Why, with some noble exceptions, have American universities become so intellectually closed? A few reasons suggest themselves.

First, there is no accountability. Professors are not held accountable for their ideas, no matter how foolish, or even evil, those ideas might be. This disastrous freedom from accountability exists only in academia. If a businessman believes and espouses enough foolish ideas, his business will fail. If I regularly espoused foolish ideas on my radio show, callers would make mincemeat of them, and I would eventually lose credibility, listeners, and my job. But when a professor regularly repeats foolish ideas, he is hardly ever answerable for his words or for the failures emanating from them – e.g., the abject failure of bilingual education for immigrant children, or the partisan obstruction of the American principle of free speech and the academic principle of intellectual freedom.

Second, a monolithic ideological blanket covers most universities. There is little or no intellectual challenge to professors on the Left. Peruse the books assigned in most liberal arts classes and ask yourself this question: Are diverse points of view offered? The answer, unfortunately, will in most instances be no. Then listen in on lectures and class discussion. As Heather McCormick, a moderate Democrat, observes in "The Unprofitable Monopoly," "many who disagree with the ultra-liberal viewpoint that dominates discussion at Boalt have learned to keep silent." Consequently, "expectations are anchored so far to the Left at Boalt" that "in most classes, we don't hear from true conservatives at all, only less extreme liberals." Similarly, outside speakers invited to lecture at universities or to give commencement addresses almost never represent opinions not endorsed by the Left. Which raises a further question: Who is going to challenge the average politically correct professor of the Left? An intimidated student with a question in class?

Third, there is, in my view, one particularly disastrous consequence to the direction taken by the American university during the last thirty years – a lack of belief in the value of traditional wisdom. The amount of nonsense believed by university intellectuals on the radical Left in the twentieth century is not matched by any other mainstream group. Only they have believed in Marxism; only they believe that truth doesn't exist; that no text means anything and can be deconstructed to mean everything; that Beethoven wrote Dead White European music, not eternal and universal music. And the list of such foolish, and often dangerous, ideas goes on.

Fourth, the contemporary university is generally a fundamentalist secular seminary. Its view of life is as one-dimensional as a fundamentalist religious seminary's view of life. But there is a big difference. Whereas every religious seminary openly acknowledges that it has one way to view the world — through religious eyes — the secular university tells the world that it has no set way in which to view the world, that it is nonpartisan and intellectually open. But universities are, by and large, no longer intellectually open. The most fundamentalist seminary is therefore more intellectually honest about its aims than your average American university.

As *The Diversity Hoax* makes abundantly clear, the newest false god of the university is "diversity." It emanates from the race-based radicalism that permeates academic life. The belief that diversity, when defined solely by race and ethnicity, is meaningful is, of course, a racist idea. Many universities actually support the belief that skin color is significant, such that any combination of people from various races and ethnicities constitutes a diverse group – even if in truth those people think identically. In other words, like the classic racists we rightly condemn, believers in the current doctrine of "diversity" suggest that race is more important than character or thought. Some even suggest that race does determine character and thought.

In nearly every generation, unfortunately, the battle for truth, decency, and tolerance is waged by a minority. Thus, the battle to return truth-seeking and civility to the American university is being waged by a few students who, no matter what their actual politics, are regularly dismissed as conservatives, fascists, racists, sexists, or members of the Christian Right (even those of us who are Jews have been branded as such).

David Wienir, Marc Berley, and the contributors to *The Diversity Hoax* are profiles in courage. They are the shepherds among mostly sheep.

While the battle for good has almost always pitted the few against the many, what is new – and disturbing – is that for the first time in American history the forces arrayed against truth and moral norms are centered in the university. This means that foolish and often dangerous ideas are placed into the mouths of our children, and our children are graded on how well they can repeat them.

Whether American society can survive an assault on its basic values from its intellectual elite remains to be seen. But *The Diversity Hoax* gives us hope. There are doubtless many other students who think what the students in this book are saying. Perhaps this collection of essays will give some college and university students the courage to speak their real thoughts on these matters. If it does, perhaps high school students will soon again have reason to thumb university catalogues with a youthful excitement about learning.

Dennis Prager
Los Angeles, California
January, 1999

Dennis Prager is one of America's most respected radio talk show hosts. His nationally syndicated show broadcasts from KABC Radio in Los Angeles. He is also a Jewish theologian and best-selling author whose books include Think a Second Time *(HarperCollins) and* Happiness Is a Serious Problem *(HarperCollins). You may visit him at www.dennisprager.com.*

Appendices

APPENDIX A

Proposition 209

(a) The state shall not discriminate against, or grant preferential treatment to, any individual or group on the basis of race, sex, color, ethnicity, or national origin in the operation of public employment, public education, or public contracting.

(b) This section shall apply only to action taken after the section's effective date.

(c) Nothing in this section shall be interpreted as prohibiting bona fide qualifications based on sex which are reasonably necessary to the normal operation of public employment, public education, or public contracting.

(d) Nothing in this section shall be interpreted as invalidating any court order or consent decree which is in force as of the effective date of this section.

(e) Nothing in this section shall be interpreted as prohibiting action which must be taken to establish or maintain eligibility for any federal program, where ineligibility would result in a loss of federal funds to the state.

(f) For the purposes of this section, "state" shall include, but not necessarily be limited to, the state itself, any city, county, city and county, public university system, including the University of California, community college district, school district, special district, or any other political subdivision or governmental instrumentality of or within the state.

(g) The remedies available for violations of this section shall be the same, regardless of the injured party's race, sex, color, ethnicity, or national origin, as are otherwise available for violations of then-existing California antidiscrimination law.

(h) This section shall be self-executing. If any part or parts of this section are found to be in conflict with federal law or the United State Constitution, the section shall be implemented to the maximum extent that federal law and the United States Constitution permit. Any provision held invalid shall be severable from the remaining portions of this section.

APPENDIX B

 Foundation for
Academic Standards
& Tradition

Who we are

College and university students from across the political spectrum
share one concern – they know they are not getting the rigorous,
broad liberal arts education they deserve. The students of FAST are
bright, reasonable, free-thinking young people who know that too
much of their education – and future – is being compromised by sys-
temic "dumbing down" and irresponsible politicization by many of
their professors.

One member, a young woman who is a Princeton student, wrote:

*I am worried that learning today at the college level is confined to
present-day problems and writers and lacks the emphasis on classi-
cal literature that provides the foundation for our culture. Without
studying the great works, we can hardly understand the framework
of our own society.*

Another member, a Yale sophomore, had this to say about FAST:

*Though a self-confessed bleeding-heart liberal, I am sympathetic to
FAST's goals because I feel liberalism can only be understood as part*

*of the Western tradition (even Marx is a dead white man!) and that
political correctness is a break with the left's tradition of respecting
the freedom of the individual.*

Intellectual freedom, academic standards, individual rights, and the
value of the Western tradition are enormous concerns for countless
college students. The students of FAST are standing up to make the
changes they know are necessary to ensure their future.

The dedicated and energetic students of FAST are the wonderful future of America.

OUR MISSION

FAST is a not-for-profit organization created to empower diverse
college and university students nationwide to restore both high academic standards and humanistic study of the liberal arts in the
Western tradition. FAST supports broad traditional core requirements and works to reverse the tragic "dumbing down" and radical
politicization in evidence at so many schools, even America's elite
colleges.

Students must be at the center of any movement to raise academic standards, especially at the college level. By organizing and
insisting that schools once again commit themselves to pursuing
excellence, students will be able to secure for themselves and future
generations of Americans the kind of education that life in the
twenty-first century will demand.

The need

The future of America depends on the quality of its education. But,
as countless studies show, our schools – and those who run them –
are failing in many ways. Too many students graduate from
American colleges without acquiring basic skills such as reading crit-
ically and writing clearly, and too many elite colleges are failing truly
to challenge their best students. At an education summit in 1997,
various corporate presidents spoke about the failure of America's
schools to prepare students for the workplace, and they expressed significant worries about our country's future.

Unfortunately, even while these leaders talk about the need to improve education, educators and administrators continue to move college curricula away from traditional subjects that teach basic skills – especially in the humanities. Rather than raise standards, teachers and administrators continue to lower them. To take just one example, as *The New Republic* reported last year, of 70 elite colleges surveyed by the National Alumni Forum two out of three do not require a course in Shakespeare for a major in English. At Georgetown, as *The New York Times* reported, students are instead encouraged to take courses in which they get credit for writing about television shows or other elements of popular culture.

Even at schools where Shakespeare is included, his works are increasingly taught from an irresponsibly narrow or radically politicized perspective – frequently with a perverse, unenlightening focus on race, class, and gender. Such irresponsibility cheats countless students. The most useful and appropriate approach for undergraduates is still the traditional study of Shakespeare's dramatic art and human insight. But this valuable, traditional emphasis is quickly disappearing from college classrooms across the country.

Today, humanities courses such as English and history are most widely affected, but so are courses in science and mathematics, as well as many other subjects, as recent poor performances by American students in international competitions and rankings show.

Founded in 1996, FAST was created because students are concerned about declining standards and worried about their futures.

FAST is dedicated to helping students effect the changes in their colleges and universities that will give their education real value and best prepare them for the competitive American workplace and life itself.

WHAT WE ARE DOING

- Organizing students on college and university campuses around the country, helping them to voice their concerns about their education and turn their concerns into effective actions for change. Ready to join us in this necessary cause? Contact us at: Students@gofast.org

- Publishing FAST's national student e-journal, *ARGOS*. Students contribute articles, participating in a civil and productive dialogue about the problems in education that most affect them. If you would like to write for *ARGOS*, contact us at: ARGOS@gofast.org

- Publishing FAST Education News, delivering education news that matters. If you have the stuff to be a FAST correspondent, or just a tip about news on your campus, contact us at: EdNews@gofast.org

- Bringing engaging speakers to college and university campuses. If you would like to bring a speaker to your school or would like yourself to become a FAST speaker, contact us at: Events@gofast.org

- Publishing Standing FAST, a newsletter that delivers the latest news about FAST to all of our members, reporting on the ways students, parents, and teachers are working together to make classrooms throughout the country places where excellence is the only goal. Do you have news you think we should cover? Contact us at: StandingFAST@gofast.org

- Working to establish the FAST Tutoring Network, in which FAST members tutor students who need help in reading, math, history, science, and other subjects. If you would like to become a FAST Tutor, contact us at: Tutor@gofast.org

FAST is a 501(c)(3) not-for-profit organization.
All donations are tax-deductible.

APPENDIX C

THE FEDERALIST SOCIETY STATEMENT OF PURPOSE

"The Courts must declare the sense of the law; and if they should be disposed to exercise WILL instead of JUDGEMENT the consequence would be the substitution of their pleasure to that of the legislative body."

The Federalist No. 78

Purpose

Law schools and the legal profession are currently strongly dominated by a form of orthodox liberal ideology which advocates a centralized and uniform society. While some members of the academic community have dissented from these views, by and large they are taught simultaneously with (and indeed as if they were) the law.

The Federalist Society for Law and Public Policy Studies is a group of conservatives and libertarians interested in the current state of the legal order. It is founded on the principles that the state exists to preserve freedom, that the separation of governmental powers is central to our Constitution, and that it is emphatically the province and duty of the judiciary to say what the law is, not what the law should be. The Society seeks both to promote an awareness of these principles and to further their application through its activities.

This entails reordering priorities within the legal system to place a premium on individual liberty, traditional values, and the rule of law. It also requires restoring the recognition of the importance of these norms among lawyers, judges, and law professors. In working to achieve these goals, the Society has created a conservative intellectual network that extends to all levels of the legal community.

APPENDIX D

A MEMORANDUM FROM THE DEAN

Memorandum

To: The Boalt Community

From: Dean Herma Hill Kay

Re: Student Organization Flyers and Bulletin Boards

Date: April 3, 1998

In recent weeks, certain student organizations' flyers have been torn down from bulletin boards around Boalt Hall, and, in one instance, a student organization's own bulletin board has been defaced. We do not know who is responsible for these acts, and we hope that Boalt students are not involved. I write to remind the entire community that such acts of disrespect not only threaten the academic environment, which can thrive only when ideas are freely exchanged and encouraged, but also violate Boalt Hall and UC campus policies and regulations. As everyone should know, our policy is that properly posted flyers should be left in place and bulletin boards should not be disturbed – it is incumbent upon all members of this community to comply with these policies. We must all be committed to protecting the freedom of our students and our student groups and to fostering an atmosphere of mutual respect in which intelligent and reasoned discourse will prevail over efforts to exclude some voices from the debate.

If you have any information about the tearing down of flyers or the defacement of bulletin boards, I urge you to contact Assistant Dean Leslie Oster or Jody Knower, Director of Student Life Services, immediately.

ACKNOWLEDGEMENTS

The editors express their deepest thanks to the following people for their help in the making of this book: Andrew Armstrong, Brian W. Jones, Jodie Langel, Herbert London, Steve Marmer, Miwa Messer, Charles E. Mercier, Eve Piscina, Vered R. Sussman, and Gilbert K. Zachary.

James Robie devoted his talent and time to designing this book, and the editors express their deepest appreciation and thanks. Kevin Goering provided far more than counsel, for which the editors are extremely grateful.

The editors thank their families for their loving encouragement. Finally, to the contributors, the editors express their admiration.

FAST thanks the Argosy Foundation for its support.

About the Editors

DAVID WIENIR is a member of the class of 2000 at the University of California, Berkeley School of Law (Boalt Hall). He is co-author of *Last Time: Labour's Lessons from the Sixties* (London: Bellew Press, 1997) with Austin Mitchell, Member of British Parliament (Labour, Great Grimsby). He graduated from Columbia University in 1995 with a B.A. in political science and studied history and politics at Oxford University as a visiting scholar. He earned his M.Sc. in Public Administration and Public Policy from the London School of Economics in 1996. David has worked as an intern for the Los Angeles District Attorney; hosted a political and cultural commentary broadcast on Estonia National Radio in the former Soviet Union; worked as researcher within the British House of Commons; conducted research for the Survivors of the Shoah Visual History Foundation; and worked for the Governor of California's Legal Affairs Office.

MARC BERLEY is executive director of the Foundation for Academic Standards & Tradition (FAST), a not-for-profit organization created to empower diverse college and university students nationwide to restore high academic standards and humanistic study of the liberal arts in the Western tradition to their schools. He earned his Ph.D. in English and Comparative Literature from Columbia University in 1993. He has taught literature, humanities, and writing at Columbia University, Lawrence University, and Rutgers University and written on Shakespeare, Milton, Plato, W. B. Yeats, Wallace Stevens, and education.